THE BHS COMPLETE MANUAL OF
EQUITATION

The British Horse Society

THE BHS COMPLETE MANUAL OF EQUITATION

The Training of Horse and Rider

Consultant Editor

Patrick Print OBE FBHS

KENILWORTH PRESS

Copyright © 2011 The British Horse Society

Some material first published in the UK in 1982 in *The BHS Manual of Equitation*
by Kenilworth Press, an imprint of Quiller Publishing Ltd
Second edition 2001
This edition published 2011
Reprinted 2013

British Library Cataloguing-in-Publication Data
A catalogue record for this book
is available from the British Library

ISBN 978 1 905693 37 5

Line drawings by Dianne Breeze
Cover and book design by Sharyn Troughton

Printed in Malta by Gutenberg Press Ltd.

Kenilworth Press

An imprint of Quiller Publishing
Wykey House, Wykey, Shrewsbury, SY4 1JA
Tel: 01939 261616 Fax: 01939 261606
E-mail: info@quillerbooks.com
Website: www.kenilworthpress.co.uk

Contents

# Preface

THE BRITISH HORSE SOCIETY'S *COMPLETE MANUAL OF EQUITATION* is based on the classical lines first written about by Xenophon (430–354 BC) maintained by the Spanish Riding School in Vienna and now amended for competitions by the *Fédération Equestre Internationale*.

Whilst it is difficult, if not impossible, to lay down hard and fast rules on the training of the horse and rider, and horsemastership in general, the *Complete Manual of Equitation* is a consensus of opinion of the national authorities and represents the general view in Britain of equitation and horsemastership. This book is the result of many eminent members of the British Horse Society devoting a good deal of time voluntarily to discussing and writing about the subject.

The first *Manual of Equitation* was edited by Jane Kidd and Barbara Slane Fleming FBHS: the second edition was revised and updated by Islay Auty FBHS. This new edition has been carefully revised and updated with contributions from the following:

Yogi Briesner FBHS – a former international event rider who represented his native country of Sweden, Yogi has been based in the UK for many years and was a previous Chairman of the then BHS Training and Education Committee. Yogi is one of the world's best-known trainers of event riders, having being GB's official team trainer for a number of years, during which time he has led GB riders to many international successes at World, Olympic and European level. He is a past recipient of The Queen's Award for Equestrianism.

Carole Broad FBHS – currently Chief Instructor of The Huntley School of Equitation near Gloucester, Vice Chairman of The British Horse Society, BHS Chief Assessor and Examinations Representative on the BHS Q & T Committee.

Jane Goldsmith FBHS – in her youth a successful competition rider, Jane was formerly Chairman of the (then) BHS Training and Education Committee. She has served as a Trustee of the BHS and is now one of the world's most respected trainers of para dressage riders and is one of the world's most highly qualified para dressage judges. She was awarded the Dressage Award at the 2010 Animal Health Trust UK Equestrian Awards.

Judy Harvey FBHS – an international dressage rider, trainer and judge. Judy has successfully trained many dressage and event riders to the highest level.

Sabrina Jones FBHS – formerly the proprietor of Laughton Manor Equestrian Centre and currently a BHS Chief Assessor and a member of the BHS Qualifications and Training Committee, Sabrina was a successful eventer and has competed internationally at dressage.

Patrick Print FBHS – Formerly BHS Scottish National Coach in the 1980s, Patrick is a freelance trainer, training many candidates for BHS exams and also competition riders. He is a BHS Chief Assessor, Member of the British Equestrian Federation Council and was Chairman of The British Horse Society from 2004 to 2010. He has previously chaired many committees, notably the BHS Training and Education Committee.

Jo Winfield FBHS – a freelance trainer, BHS Chief Assessor and current Chairman of the BHS Qualification and Training Committee. Jo is also a BE accredited trainer, a BD listed dressage judge and a part-time lecturer at Hartpury College.

The book is illustrated by Dianne Breeze.

About this Book

THIS BOOK IS DIVIDED INTO TWO PARTS: Training the Rider and Training the Horse. Inevitably, though, the two parts are interlinked, as it is impossible to learn to ride and progress without becoming involved in the way the horse moves, develops, improves and thinks.

Readers are therefore invited to dip into both parts of the book, referring back and forth for specific advice on training, be it for rider or horse, or both. The clear chapter headings and the comprehensive index will allow readers to move around the book easily, finding all the information they need to take their riding and the training of their horse forward to a higher level.

Riders wanting to learn more about related subjects such as saddlery, bitting and specialist care of the competition horse should refer to the companion volume – *The BHS Complete Manual of Horse and Stable Management* – which deals with these matters in some depth.

Introduction and Historical Review

IN THE LAST 2,500 YEARS MUCH HAS BEEN WRITTEN ABOUT THE 'ART' OF EQUITATION. Whilst there is clear evidence of riding in central Asia dating from the second millennium BC, one of the earliest and best-known treatises was written much later by the Greek general, Xenophon. His book *The Art of Horsemanship* was written in approximately 350 BC. Xenophon refers throughout his work to Simon of Athens and so it is very likely that the subject had been written about before. However, unlike any other narratives which may have been written two or more millennia ago, Xenophon's work is the only work of such antiquity to have been preserved intact.

Many of the old classical masters refer to equitation as an art and a science. Today it is often referred to as a sport. It must be remembered, however, that (other than racing) riding as a competitive sport has only really evolved in the last 100 years or so. Before this the horse was used primarily in combat, or as a means of conveyance for hunting, or for transport, as well as a means of educating noblemen of the royal courts of Europe in the 'finer arts'.

One trend which does appear to have emerged is that all the old masters' writings were governed by the use of the horse in their period. However, what is for sure is that the horse has not changed in essence over the centuries and many of the writings and teachings of our predecessors, particularly those who advocated humane principles, still hold true today no matter what the horse is being used for.

Nowadays we have clear documentary evidence of the practice of equitation through the modern technology of film and video. Moreover, modern veterinary understanding means that our reasons for doing something are now underpinned by science. One therefore wonders whether some of the masters of yesteryear were any better than today. After all, we only have their word for it! What is clear, however, is that some of the past masters' writings, when followed studiously, have time and again provided clear, humane directions for the training of the horse no matter what his use.

Some would argue that practice alone is all that is needed to progress in equitation. However any sensible horseman would advise that a sound theoretical understanding can not only enhance one's proficiency but also minimise the risk of the welfare of the horse being compromised. (And don't forget, you can practice a mistake a hundred times until you can commit that mistake perfectly…)

As de la Guérinière quite rightly observed: 'Every science and every art has its own principles and rules that lead to new discoveries and perfection. Why should horsemanship be the only art for which practice alone is needed?'

François Robichon de la Guérinière (1688–1751) was born in France and was a student of Antoine de Vendeuil. In 1731 he published his book *Ecole de Cavalerie (School of Horsemanship)*. This was to become one of the most important works on equitation. Not only is it clear that he advocates improving the horse through education rather than coercion; his work is logically and simply written, leaving the reader in no doubt as to the progression of the training of the horse. It is widely accepted that he invented the very important movement of 'shoulder-in'. However there is evidence that this invention was based on the ideas of an Englishman, William Cavendish, Duke of Newcastle (1592–1676) expressed almost a century earlier in his work *A General System of Horsemanship.*

There is no doubt that de la Guérinière's work has had one of the most profound influences on modern day equitation. Certainly, it is considered that the methods and practices of the Spanish Riding School are based on his principles.

A century and a half later Gustav Steinbrecht (1808–1885) came to prominence. Steinbrecht was a student of Louis Seeger (1798–1865) who was a pupil of Max von Weyrother, the famous Oberbereiter from Vienna. Steinbrecht wrote another influential work, *Das Gymnasium des Pferdes (The Gymnasium of the Horse)*. This book, published posthumously, goes directly back to de la Guérinière and is considered to be the basis of all equitation in Germany. The German cavalry of the early twentieth century considered this work their 'bible' and published a cavalry manual, updated annually, based on its principles. In the 1912 edition we find the first clear directives of what are now known as the 'Scales of Training' (see Chapter 11).

About the same period as Steinbrecht, François Baucher (1796–1873) practised his 'art' in the circus of Laurent and Adolphe Franconi in the Champs Elysée, Paris. Whilst Steinbrecht produced horses for the circus using classical methods, Baucher did not. Some of the movements he produced were considered unnatural – canter backwards and canter on three legs were just two of the eccentricities he encouraged. Many attribute the invention of the flying change of leg at every stride (one-time changes) to him. Although he wrote his first book in 1833 it was not until 1842 that his most important work was produced, his *Method d' equitation*. This became known as his 'first method' to distinguish it from the 1874 revision of the text by Faverot de Kerbrech (the 'second method'). What is the difference? In the first method he was considered by many to be quite forceful. Much work advocated standing still with direct flexions of the head and neck of the horse with severe bits, and the training of the horse was quite hurried, using harsh methods which broke the horse's will.

Baucher mellowed with age; perhaps his accident in 1855 in which a heavy chandelier fell on him was a contributory factor. As a result his 'second method' advocated taking more time, schooling the horse in motion and a calmer, more humane approach. There is no doubt that Baucher was a genius if only for his ability to ride a horse with lightness or, as the French would say, with légèreté. His methods varied greatly from the German/Viennese school. However he still has his followers today.

The Complete Training of Horse and Rider by Alois Podhajsky was published in 1967 and was considered a modern masterpiece. Col Podhajsky was Director of the Spanish Riding School and in his work he advocates a simple step by step guide to training the horse using correct classical methods. In his work Podhajsky clearly states that 'theory without practice is of little value, whereas practice is the proof of theory' and 'knowledge must always take precedence over action'. Many still consider this book to be the 'bible' of equitation.

Podhajsky's book was one of several written in the twentieth century with direct links to the masters of before. Waldemar Seunig's *Horsemanship* (published in Germany in 1941 and in Britain in 1956) and Wilhelm Müseler's *Riding Logic* (first published in1937) were very much of the German School whilst *Reflections on Equestrian Art* by the Portuguese master Nuno Oliveira (published in Britain in1976) gives a delightful insight into the work of this talented artist who advocates in some part the principles of Baucher albeit according to Baucher's second manner and on humane terms.

Not until the beginning of the twentieth century was there anything of real value written on the performance of the horse over fences. It was not until Piero Santini put into words the methods of the Italian Cavalry Officer Federico Caprilli in his book *The Forward Impulse* (published 1937) that we have anything of classical value on this subject. Later, Anthony Paalman's *Training Showjumpers* (1978) is, in the author's words, based on the 'natural training methods evolved from the principles of the European Classical Schools'.

There has been over time many excellent works by lesser lights and here into the twenty-first century masters evolve and some have put down their principles and methods into words and, as has been suggested before, modern technology will enable us to have a truly lasting and accurate insight into their training of the horse. There will always be disagreements over methods but only through educated discussion can the principles of classical riding be preserved to protect the welfare of the horse in future generations.

Whilst not intending to compete with the writings of past masters this book is intended as a simple guide for riders and instructors of all levels. It is meant to be a step by step guide written in simple terms relevant to the twenty-first century. The authors of the various chapters are all Fellows of The British Horse Society who themselves can trace their equestrian pedigree back to those masters of yesteryear.

If the welfare of the horse is not to be compromised then this book should be read in conjunction with *The British Horse Society's Complete Manual of Horse and Stable Management.*

PART 1

TRAINING THE RIDER

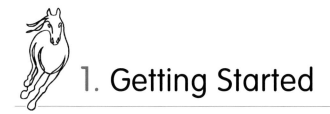

1. Getting Started

Learning to ride

RIDING IS A SPORTING ACTIVITY THAT REQUIRES A UNIQUE APPROACH compared to other sports as it not only demands a physical ability to develop the necessary riding skills but also a psychological understanding of working with a live and intelligent animal. The joy of being able to work with horses allows us to be able to take up this activity as children or as adults, and the uniqueness of the horse allows us to continue long into our maturity as active riders within a variety of activities including:

- Hacking and pleasure riding
- Riding Club activities
- Dressage
- Show jumping
- Eventing
- BHS Trec (orienteering combined with cross-country riding and obedience tests)
- Endurance riding
- Showing in hand and under saddle

When someone wants to start to ride it is important for them to consider why they wish to become involved with horses and to understand the commitment that this takes in order to get the best experience and companionship from riding and working with horses. Initially, what is necessary to get started is a good attitude, and some helpful advice and support.

The most sensible place to start is through an approved British Horse Society (BHS) Establishment. Details of centres in the locality are most easily found through the BHS website, listings of which can be found through regional areas, which also indicate the type of training and levels of riders that each centre can support. Training at an approved centre will guarantee that a rider will be supported by well trained and qualified staff.

BRITISH HORSE SOCIETY EXAMINATION SYSTEM

STAGE ONE

EQL LEVEL 1 CERTIFICATE IN BHS RIDING HORSES

Riding horses on the flat and over ground poles in the light seat

EQL LEVEL 1 CERTIFICATE IN BHS HORSE KNOWLEDGE AND CARE

Brushing off horses including putting on and taking off equipment
Horse husbandry, identification and handling
The principles of caring for horses

STAGE TWO

EQL LEVEL 2 DIPLOMA IN BHS RIDING HORSES

EQL Level 2 Certificate in Riding Horses on the Flat
Ride horses on the flat in an enclosed area
Ride horses over fences in an enclosed area

EQL LEVEL 2 DIPLOMA IN BHS HORSE KNOWLEDGE AND CARE

EQL Level 2 Certificate in Horse Care
Groom and plait horses and fit equipment
The principles of horse health and anatomy
The principles of shoeing, clipping and trimming horses
Fit, remove and maintain tack for exercise
Lunge a horse under supervision

EQL Level 2 Award in the Principles of Horse Care
The principles of stabling and grassland care for horses
The principles of watering, feeding and fittening horses

STAGE THREE

EQL LEVEL 3 DIPLOMA IN BHS RIDING HORSES

EQL Level 3 Certificate in Riding Horses on the Flat
Ride horses on the flat
Ride horses over fences

EQL LEVEL 3 DIPLOMA IN BHS HORSE KNOWLEDGE AND CARE

EQL Level 3 Certificate in Horse Care
Fit tack and equipment, and care for the competition horse
Horse health, anatomy and physiology
Lunge a fit horse for exercise

EQL Level 3 Award in the Principles of Horse Care
The principles of feeding and fittening horses
The principles of stabling and grassland care for horses

To achieve the BHSAI a candidate must be successful in L3 BHS Riding Horses, L3 BHS Horse Knowledge and Care, BHS Preliminary Teaching of Horse Riding and complete a portfolio.

STAGE FOUR

BHS STAGE 4 IN RIDING HORSES ON THE FLAT

BHS STAGE 4 IN RIDING HORSES OVER FENCES

BHS STAGE 4 IN LUNGEING

Intermediate Teaching, consisting of:
Teaching riding on the flat up to BD Elementary
Teaching riding over fences, show jumping or cross-country
Teaching an improving rider on the lunge
Class lesson, either flat or grid work
Deliver a presentation
Theory covering business knowledge and teaching

To achieve BHSII a candidate must be successful in both the Stage 4 and Intermediate Teaching Test

To achieve the BHSI the candidate must be successful in BHS Stable Manager, BHS Senior Coach and BHS Equitation

RIDING AND ROAD SAFETY

EQL LEVEL 2 AWARD IN BHS RIDING HORSES SAFELY ON THE PUBLIC HIGHWAY

The principles of riding horses on the highway
Ride a horse in a enclosed area and on the highway

COACHING

EQL LEVEL 3 CERTIFICATE IN BHS PRELIMINARY TEACHING OF HORSE RIDING

Coach a group of riders for improvement
Coach an inexperienced rider for improvement

EQL Level 2 Award in the Principles of Coaching Sport
Understanding the fundamentals of coaching sport
Understanding how to develop participants
through coaching sport
Supporting participants' lifestyle through
coaching sport
Understanding the principles of safe and
equitable coaching practice

For information on UKCC Endorsed Coaching Awards and Certificates please contact the Exams Office directly for information.

Each centre will have a minimum of one registered BHS Instructor which means that they have a recognised first aid qualification and undertake regular training sessions themselves in order to stay up to date with their own education, alongside well-trained and cared for horses. Every centre undergoes regular inspections to confirm the quality and consistency of the training provision. In addition to this standard, the approval means that the centre holds a Local Authority Licence, which includes the appropriate insurance cover and health care assessment of the horses.

The riding school

Every centre has different facilities: most will have an outdoor riding area on an artificial surface with allows riding to take place most of the year. Some centres will also have an indoor school which will allow riding all year round and this can be a valuable asset in the winter months and in inclement weather. A visual assessment of the establishment will tell a lot about the centre; the yard should be tidy and clean, with an organised feeling about the stables. The fields should be tidy and free from rubbish and weeds. The size of the centre does not reflect the quality of provision that it can offer; some smaller establishments can provide a more consistent one-to-one training opportunity than the bigger centres with many instructors. It is therefore important that an individual considers the type of environment, the atmosphere and the commitment that a centre can offer before deciding where to train.

Once a choice of centre has been made, the individual will need to contact the centre and arrange an appointment either to visit, or to book an initial assessment lesson. The centre should, at this stage, inform the potential client of their policies and how to book a lesson, and acquire the basic information that they will need in order to provide a safe and suitable horse. It is important at this stage that the client has a discussion with the centre about what their aims and expectations are. This way both client and centre can plan ahead knowing what the timescale is for achieving these goals as well as being able to establish a budget for the training and discuss factors such as motivation.

Every centre will take personal details in order to manage any risk to the client and to support their individual needs: they will need to know age, height, weight and any medical information that should be provided in order to manage health and safety factors whilst riding. This information is important in order to cover any health concerns that may need to be managed in order to look after a client in the event of an accident – e.g. an asthmatic may need an inhaler and should make that information available when booking a lesson and can then carry the necessary medical inhaler with them (or in close proximity) when riding.

Other concerns include any previous medical injury that may impact upon an individual's ability to ride, such as a back complaint or previously broken bones that may limit movement – e.g. to an ankle. Such information and awareness are needed in order that the instructor can not only select the right horse for the client but can also help in establishing the correct position whilst being aware of any physical limitations that may make some aspects harder to establish.

Instructors

In equestrian terminology, the word 'instructor' has been inherited from the old cavalry schools and, while less relevant to the modern world, the terminology has stayed within this industry. Within the qualifications that the BHS offers, various levels of instructor are available to provide training and education to riders. Within the first level of teaching qualification, there is the BHS Assistant Instructor which incorporates the United Kingdom Coaching Qualification (UKCC) at Level Two; this is the equivalent of a Sport Level Two Coach, and so the terms instructor and coach may be used within this training environment. The main priority is that the individual is a registered BHS Instructor, which provides reassurance that they remain current in their training and education to provide the best that they can offer in terms of knowledge and understanding of the requirements for supporting the clients who are learning to ride. Regardless of the title given to the person providing the training, they should be good communicators, enabling clients to develop the skills that they require to meet their training needs.

Clothing

Riding is a risk sport and as such requires a certain amount of personal protective equipment. The most important investment for any rider is a suitable appropriately fitted riding hat. Some riding schools will allow a beginner rider to hire a hat in their initial lessons; these centres will have been trained in the selection and fit of this equipment so that safety needs can be met. Once a client has decided that they wish to continue learning to ride then it is advisable that they purchase their own riding hat that conforms to the following safety kite marks:

- PAS 015
- EN 1384
- ASTM F1163
- BSEN 1384
- SNELL E2001

Suitable footwear is another important consideration for safety. Short jodhpur boots are ideal and can initially be worn with trousers, tracksuit, or ideally jodhpurs; additionally they become more comfortable if worn with half chaps (leggings that go over the boot and secure around the lower leg underneath the knee). Jodhpurs or breeches are specialist trousers that are most suitable for riding as they provide a good fit and comfort whilst riding. If jodhpur boots are not available then sensible walking shoes may be suitable provided they have a flat sole and a small heel. Trainers are not suitable because of the lack of heel and the possibility that they can slip through the stirrup and trap the rider's foot. Wellington boots are also unsuitable, because of their width and thick ridged soles. Whatever clothes are worn, they need to be safe and comfortable in all seasons so the following recommendations should be considered.

- Warm layers in winter, thicker gloves and socks when the temperature gets cold.

- Lightweight layers in warmer weather.

- Waterproof jacket for riding outside.

- Gloves – to protect the hands all year round.

- Clothing should be loose-fitting for comfort but should be secured – nothing undone that can flap about and either worry the horse or get caught up in the tack.

- Avoid loose clothes, scarves, jewellery, etc. as these can be a dangerous when around the horse.

Motivation and fitness

As riding is an active sport, any basic fitness that may have been developed through general activities (such as swimming, dog-walking, cycling) will help in developing the skills and coordination for riding more quickly. We all ride for a variety reasons and when we initially start in this sport it is quite normal to use muscles that haven't had to work in the same way before. It is usual to experience some degree of muscle soreness when learning to ride; this can either be part of a feeling of well-being – achieving a newly learnt skill – or be uncomfortable if a newcomer has been trying to do too much too soon.

A novice rider often takes lessons on a once-per-week basis. During the riding session the instructor should be aware of the client's fitness and consequently their ability to cope with learning newly acquired skills of balance and coordination when on a horse. In the first few lessons, frequent rest periods should be given to allow the client to recover their fitness and to reflect on how well they are progressing.

It is a good idea for a client to book in a series of lessons on a weekly basis as this will help aid motivation and provide a progressive programme to look forward as they learn the basics. Initially private lessons of 30 minutes will be the most suitable, these may start as a lead-rein or lunge lesson. Once the client has mastered the basic skills of steering in walk and trot, maintaining balance, and has developed an awareness of how to communicate with the horse they will be able to join in a class lesson. Class lessons have three or more people in them and allow those of a similar standard to learn to ride together. This is also a good way for clients to socialise and learn new skills with similar levels of riders.

Rider's body shape

Anyone is able to ride and people come in all shapes and sizes. It is important to be aware of different body shapes and how they can influence the ability to ride. People come in three main body types and these will reflect why it is easier for them to feel better and more balanced on some horses more than others. It is important that individuals know and understand their body shape and that instructors are familiar with the underlying criteria so that a suitable horse can be provided to help meet individual needs. 'Somatotype' is the word that describes the type of shape that an individual matures into; it does not reflect on fitness levels, or relate to age or gender, but refers to the shape and ratios of the natural body.

Somatotypes

Somatotypes

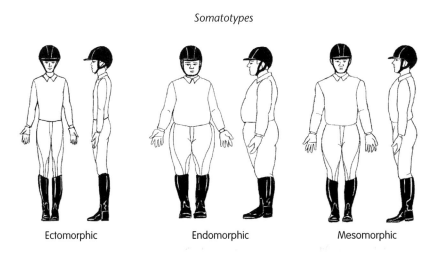

Ectomorphic   Endomorphic   Mesomorphic

- Ectomorphic is characterised by long and thin muscles/limbs and low fat storage; receding chin, usually referred to as 'slim'.

- Mesomorphic is characterised by medium bones, solid torso, low fat levels, and wide shoulders with a narrow waist; usually referred to as 'muscular'.

- Endomorphic is characterised by increased fat storage, a wide waist and a large bone structure, usually referred to as 'fat'.

Understanding natural shape will allow the instructor to choose the most suitable horse for the client and to help them adjust to a suitable position when riding. People with a slim build will have long legs and be able to ride wider-shaped horses; they will also need to ride with a longer length of stirrup leather to accommodate their position in the saddle. These riders are often long in their body ratio from knee to hip and so need a suitable saddle with enough room in the seat to accommodate their leg length.

People with a shorter, more athletic body, may need to ride with a shorter length of stirrup leather in order to accommodate their thigh shape; this type of body shape is likely to find the jumping position easier as it allows them to use the strength in their legs, although their balance may be less established. This type of body shape is best suited to narrower horses to allow the inner thigh to come into better contact with the saddle.

Regardless of body shape, it is the selection of the most suitable horse and saddle that the instructor will need to consider when a client first starts to ride and learns to establish the basic position on the flat and later when jumping. As their riding position improves, the instructor will be able to offer a greater variety of horses to ride, so that the client can work on establishing a better balance on different horses of different shapes and sizes too.

Selecting the first horse

The choice of horse a newcomer rides will firstly be dependent upon the physical details that were registered with the yard office and secondly will be related to the horse's temperament and suitability as a schoolmaster for a novice rider. Horses, like people, have personalities so it is important that the horse selected is going to be appropriate to the rider's needs as a beginner. The horse should have the following characteristics:

- Be generous in nature to accommodate poor aids (signalling) from a beginner rider.

- Have an even temperament and be sensible in nature.

- Be willing and forward-going in nature, yet calm and relaxed.

- Be basically comfortable in walk, trot and canter, so as to not throw the novice rider out of balance.

- Be relaxed when moving into and out of transitions (the changes from one gait to another).

- Be educated and familiar with the school surroundings.

- Probably a middleweight build, which is likely to make him a more comfortable ride than a very narrow or heavily built horse.

The riding arena

Many riding schools possess both indoor and outdoor arenas. As the name suggests, an indoor arena will be enclosed, with a roof, and an outdoor school will be enclosed by some kind of perimeter. Both arenas will have some kind of artificial surface on which the horses work.

Arenas for dressage competition and practice are either 20m x 40m, or 20m x 60m, and most arenas are built to these standard dimensions. Outdoor arenas may, however, be considerably larger, allowing two or more dressage arenas to be set up within the area. Increasingly, premises with these types of facility are used as regular competition venues. With the ever-increasing popularity of dressage as a sport, more and more centres offer all-weather surfaces for both working-in and competing on. These centres are favoured for the higher level of competition, where the well-being of very valuable dressage horses becomes more important. With the increase of winter competitions, again these venues become well utilised, often with monthly shows.

Arena surfaces range from the more old-fashioned and less used wood-based covering (bark or shavings) through traditional ranges of sand, to the more favoured synthetic surfaces, which are usually based on some mixture containing rubber or plastic particles.

To the inexperienced eye, the letter markers around a dressage arena seem to follow no clear pattern or system. In a standard 20m x 40m arena the markers A–F–B–M–C–H–E–K are used, with D, X and G being the 'invisible' markers on the centre line. These markers, with the addition of P–R–S–V, L and I in the larger arenas, are used to enable the rider to follow instructions in the arena. Instructors also use these markers as reference points when teaching riders to execute movements and figures; and in dressage competitions, where riders are required to fulfil a prescribed test, again the markers are used for reference.

Memorising the sequence and position of the markers can be a problem for the

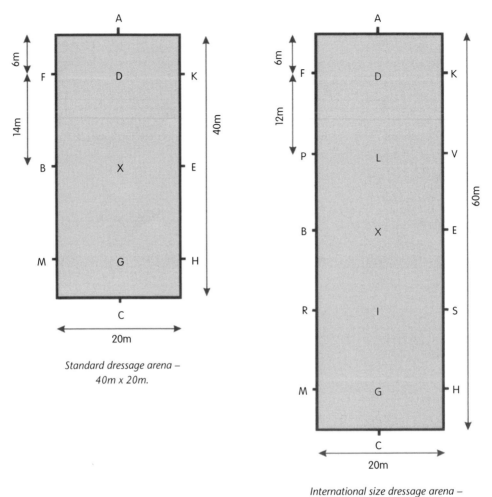

Standard dressage arena –
40m x 20m.

International size dressage arena –
60m x 20m.

beginner rider. The basic set of markers, which will be used in the training of novice riders, can be remembered by the following mnemonic:

A Fat **B**ay **M**are **C**an **H**ardly **E**ver **K**ick

Arena etiquette

A code of practice/etiquette is observed when riding in arenas, whether indoors or outside.

- Before entering or leaving the arena, other riders must be aware of your intent, so that in the interests of safety, a request to open a door or gate is known to all.

- Mounting and dismounting should take place in the centre of the arena, away from the track.

- Riders in walk should leave the outer track free for faster gaits.

- Those riding at the same gait should pass left hand to left hand, and riders using lateral work have priority on the track over basic gaits.

- Equipment such as jump-building material should be stored outside the arena or stacked safely in a corner.

The horse's basic tack

The novice rider should be familiarised with the basic equipment (or tack) that the horse will wear to be ridden. This introduction to saddlery should occur during the first riding lesson.

The novice rider's horse will wear a bridle (usually with a simple snaffle bit with a single pair of reins).

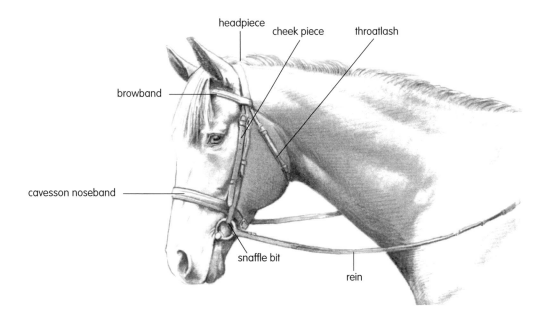

Parts of the snaffle bridle.

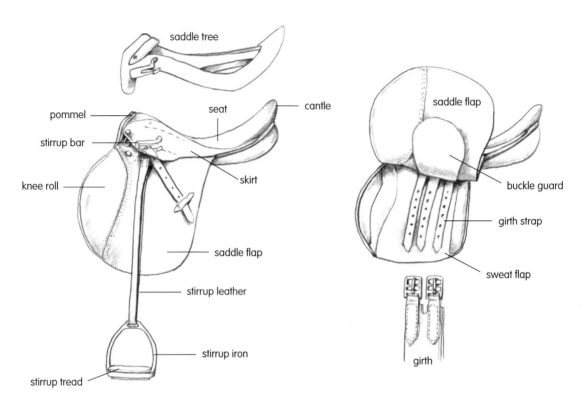

Parts of the saddle.

He will wear a saddle (usually a general-purpose saddle) which is appropriate for an inexperienced rider. (As the rider's ability develops, specialist jumping or dressage saddles may be introduced, as appropriate. These will assist attributes of position, 'feel' and security for riding in the specific disciplines.) Usually the horse will have a numnah (a soft pad) underneath the saddle to help keep him comfortable.

Often the horse will wear protective 'brushing' boots on his legs. These boots prevent an injury which could otherwise occur if the horse's legs strike into one another. Whether the horse needs one pair or two, will depend on his action.

Horses used by beginners often wear a neck strap. This is a plain leather strap that is fitted around the horse's neck. A rider who loses balance or feels unsafe can hold onto the neck strap for security and to help in regaining balance.

As the novice rider's experience and interest develop, knowledge of and familiarity with the huge range of equipment that is available for the horse will increase, whether this equipment is for day-to-day care, riding or competition.

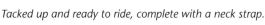

Tacked up and ready to ride, complete with a neck strap.

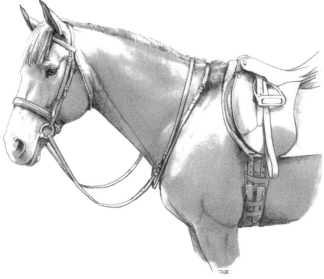

Leading the horse in hand

Knowing how to lead a horse is one of the most basic requirements for anyone who is going to ride. Learning to lead the horse should come very early in the education of the novice rider, but to begin with assistance should be given. Some riding schools encourage pupils to lead their horses from the yard or stable to the riding arena.

If leading a number of horses in a line (as in taking a group of horses out to a lesson), it is essential that each leader keeps a safe distance (about half a horse's length) from the horse in front. To be safe, each leader must be aware of what is happening in front and be ready to halt their horse or close up by increasing the speed as necessary.

When lining up a row of horses side by side ready to be mounted, it is essential to maintain a safe distance between the horses so that there is no risk of kicking or biting and possible injury to horses or riders.

The following description for leading in hand applies to a horse in a snaffle bridle:

- The bridle should be well fitted.

- The reins should be taken over the horse's head.

- The leader takes the reins in both hands, with the right hand close to the bit, and the left hand holding the remainder of the reins towards the buckled end.

- The leader should be in the vicinity of the horse's shoulder or neck, with the horse willingly stepping up alongside.

The correct way to lead a horse.

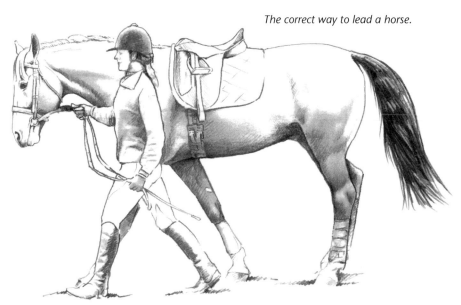

- If necessary, a whip can be carried in the leader's left hand, to be used if the horse is lazy, with a short, sharp reminder on the left flank.

- The leader should march briskly (or run if in trot), staying close to the horse, but allowing the horse to move freely without restriction by the reins.

- The leader should command the horse to 'walk on', or to 'whoa' or 'ter-rot' as required.

- A purposeful, confident manner will instil confidence and obedience in the horse.

- Authority in voice and body language will instigate submission from most horses.

Horses can be led in a headcollar or halter provided that the horse is calm, obedient, well-trained and in an off-road situation (e.g. from field to stable, or from stable to riding arena).

Mounting and dismounting

At the start of the first lesson the horse will be brought into the school for the client to mount. The first lesson may be either a lead-rein or a lunge lesson and the horse will have been tacked up with the appropriate equipment for this session. The horse can be mounted in three basic ways; mounting from the ground, by the rider being given a leg up, or from a mounting block. The last is the easiest way for a beginner.

Before the client is ready to get on, the instructor will check that the horse's tack is suitably secure and that the stirrup leathers are at an appropriate length for the rider's height and length of leg; this is done by asking the client to stand next to the horse by the saddle and by them reaching up to the top of the stirrup bar with their left hand and bringing the stirrup leather and iron towards and underneath their left arm. A standard starting length would allow the base of the stirrup to reach just underneath the rider's armpit. This is only a guideline but will be a suitable starting point. Once this length has been determined the instructor will adjust both stirrup leathers to this suitable length before bringing the horse over to the mounting block.

Mounting from a block

- The girth will have been checked, the stirrups hanging down by the saddle and the horse's reins over his head onto his neck.

- The rider picks up both of the reins in the left hand and maybe a handful of mane to give extra security, turning to face the horse's tail.

- Holding the near-side stirrup in the right hand, the rider places their left foot into it (taking care not to point their toe into the horse's side).

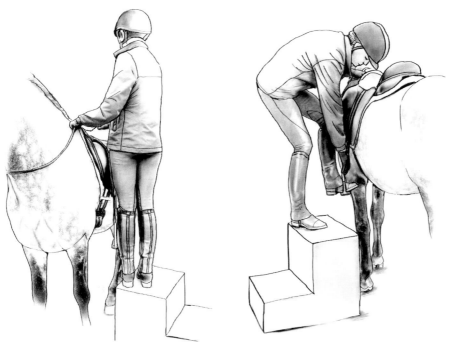

Mounting from a block.

31

Mounting from a block.

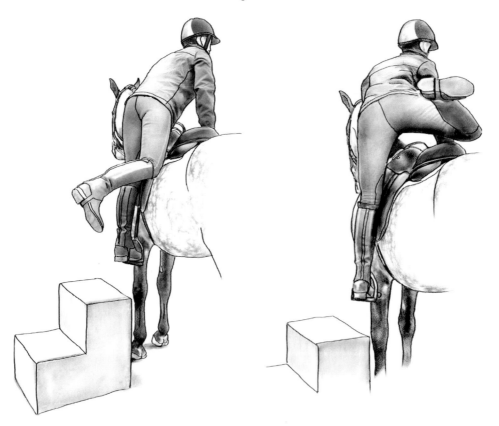

- Keeping pressure of the left foot in the stirrup, and at the same time placing their right hand on the right-hand skirt of the saddle, the rider quietly springs from the right foot, swinging the right leg over the horse's hindquarters and the cantle of the saddle.

- As the rider swings over the horse's back, they gently lower their weight onto the saddle, avoiding any excessive force landing on the saddle.

- Once sitting on the saddle, the rider places their right foot into the off-side stirrup iron.

- The suitability of the stirrups can now be checked and the rider can pick up the reins into both hands.

Time should be taken to educate the novice rider in the correct and safest way to mount; this can sometimes be overlooked but is imperative if good practice is to be established in giving riders suitable responsibility for their own care and safety.

Mounting from the ground

It is preferable to mount from a block or similar if such equipment is available. However, riders should learn to mount from the ground in case they need to if a block is not available – this requires greater agility if the rider is not to cause discomfort to the horse. Therefore, once a rider has become proficient at mounting from a raised platform (whether mounting block, raised area or small stool, then mounting from the ground can be practised. Here, additional care should be taken that the rider does not swing from the saddle in order to pull themselves up: a greater degree of athleticism is required so as not to damage the saddle or pull the horse's back, and to clear the hindquarters easily.

Mounting via a 'leg up'

Another method of mounting a horse involves being given a 'leg up' from the ground by a competent person. It is useful to watch someone else being given a 'leg up' before receiving one for the first time. There is a certain knack to the process – i.e. the two people involved need to coordinate their actions. Instructions must be clear.

Giving a 'leg up'

The person giving the 'leg up' (usually the instructor) stands close to the horse's near-side shoulder, often with one hand on the inside rein to keep the horse still. If not holding the horse, the assistant will use both hands for the 'leg up'.

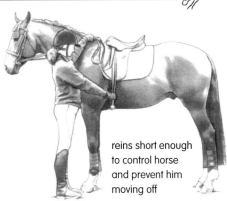

reins short enough to control horse and prevent him moving off

right hand must go well over to the off-side of the saddle

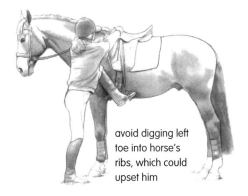

avoid digging left toe into horse's ribs, which could upset him

right leg must clear the horse's quarters athletically; weight must be lowered, with control, lightly into the saddle

Mounting from the ground.

33

The rider's left leg is lightly supported at the top of the shin, just below the knee. On the count of three or with just a slight spring from the rider, the assistant pushes the rider into the air. The lift is achieved by the rider's spring, as with the traditional method of mounting. Coordination between the rider and the assistant puts the rider cleanly into the air, and the rider then swings their right leg over the horse's hindquarters and lowers their weight into the saddle gently and with control.

This method of mounting is used throughout the racing industry where racing saddles and ultra-short stirrup leathers prevent mounting from the ground in the usual way. More often than not, young horses are taught to accept the rider being 'legged up' before they learn to cope with the rider mounting from the stirrup. Short people and children often benefit from a 'leg up'.

Receiving a 'leg up'

Unless otherwise instructed the rider should be in control of the horse to prevent him from moving. The reins (and whip if carried) should be in the left hand. (In order that the whip cannot interfere with the person giving the 'leg up', it can be held on the offside of the horse's neck.) The rider stands close to the horse, facing the saddle, with the left hand on the pommel and the right hand on the off-side of the saddle near the skirt. The left leg is bent at the knee. On the count of three, or as the rider springs into the air, a supporting push under the knee is given from the person on the ground. The right hand is released and the rider lowers their weight gently into the saddle, taking up both stirrups and adjusting the reins into both hands.

Dismounting

This is somewhat similar to the mounting process, but in reverse. The horse should be brought to a halt and required to be standing still. Initially an assistant should be available to help in this process. The rider should take both of the reins into their left hand (and if carried, the whip too) and both feet can be taken out of the stirrups. In one smooth motion the rider swings their upper body forward, simultaneously swinging their right leg backwards and up above the height of the horse's hindquarters and the cantle of the saddle. On clearing the horse's back, the rider, whilst maintaining bent knees, should land on the ground softly next to the side of the horse. Before finishing, the stirrups should be run up on both sides, the girth slackened off and the reins taken over the horse's head in order that he can then be led away safely.

2. The Rider's Basic Position on the Flat and Over Fences

THERE ARE MANY BOOKS THAT OUTLINE the perfect seat and how to apply the aids correctly. Everyone should aspire to this. However, the reality is that most riders will have some weakness and even top riders have faults that they have to concentrate on. They have people watching them on the ground most of the time, access to mirrors and videos to help them assess their faults, and the use of physios to help correct weaknesses within their body.

It is the aim of this chapter to give a basic outline of the position, concentrating on the common faults and their likely causes, so that by being aware of them we can strive to minimise the effect.

It is important for both riders and trainers to understand that often seemingly insurmountable issues can be solved by a subtle change in position.

A basic balanced seat

A correct position requires the rider to sit in the best balance possible to allow the horse to perform the work and movements required without undue stress and strain. This means that the rider must sit over the horse's centre of balance, just behind the withers, more or less over the horse's eighth rib. This is about the same place that would be comfortable if the rider were sitting bareback. It is also important to note that the rider's weight and centre of balance should be at least 10cm (4in) forward of the horse's loins in order to avoid any potential bruising to this weak area of the spine, or damage to the kidneys.

It is important to note that the rider needs to sit square on the horse and not slip to one side, being level when viewed from the front or the back. Given that most people's own build is not symmetrical, often carrying 6kg (13lb) more on one leg than the other, this is not easy but making riders aware of this problem can have its own difficulties. The head of the rider and how they carry it above their shoulders can also have an effect on the overall balance. The skull can weigh as much as 6.3kg (14lb), so riders who tend to look down to one side as they ride will upset their overall balance in both the horizontal and vertical plane.

To enable the rider to understand the requirements of their position, some practice on the ground first, without the horse, is advisable. First they should stand with their legs comfortably spread apart, approximately 60cm (2ft), with their knees slightly bent. Then they should align their upper torso above their hips and pelvis in order to find a balance in this slight squatting position. If this exercise could be practised in front of a full-length mirror the lateral balance could also be assessed and the rider would quickly feel any abnormalities in their muscle usage and coordination. Later this exercise can be developed so that the pupil stands in the same posture with their back to a wall. They should just touch the wall with the back of their head, the back of their shoulder blades, the back of their pelvis, and their heels. This will enable them to assess for themselves their vertical balance and to feel the importance of their quadriceps muscles down the front of their thighs.

Once on the horse this same muscle feeling can be replicated and the rider should be able to sit squarely in the centre of the saddle without undue tension and feel fairly balanced in order to follow the natural rhythmic movement of the horse, through their

Practising position against a wall. The rider should just touch the wall with the back of their head, shoulder blades, pelvis and heels.

The correct position for the rider, as seen from the side. Notice the ear-shoulder-hip-heel alignment.

seat and hips. This should allow the rider to be harmonious without undue extraneous movement of the limbs and torso. The rider should try to maintain two simple straight lines through their position; first, ear, shoulder, hip to heel, and second, elbow, hand, down the line of the rein to the horse's mouth. Their position should then be balanced over the horse's natural centre of balance, and allow for development of their core stability.

Outline from the side

Viewed from the side, the correct outline is shown on the previous page, with a vertical line running through the rider's ear, shoulder, hip and heel. This line remains unchanged except in the rising trot. The position of the body viewed from the side should be:

- **Head.** The rider looks straight ahead in the direction of travel, but if it is necessary to look down, this should be done with the eyes only. The head should not be dropped nor poked forward, and the jaw should not be stiff.

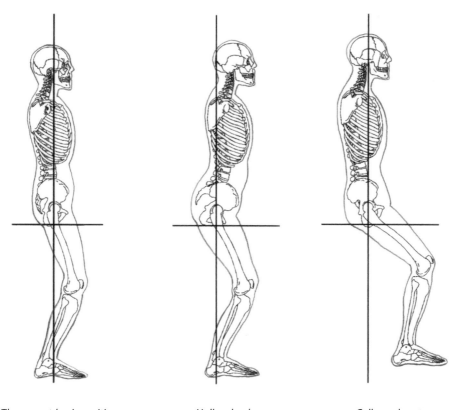

The correct basic position.   *Hollow back.*   *Collapsed seat.*

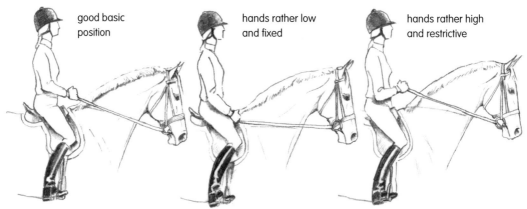

good basic
position

hands rather low
and fixed

hands rather high
and restrictive

The position of the rider's hands and arms, as seen from the side. When correct, there should be an imaginary line running from the elbow, through the wrist, to the horse's mouth.

- **Shoulders**. Should be down and well back without being stiff. This is achieved by expanding the chest rather than squaring the shoulders.

- **Back.** The body is upright, as shown on page 36 and above, with the back straight but supple. It must not be hollowed or collapsed except to the extent that it follows the natural curvature of the spine.

- **Waist.** Should not be allowed to collapse backwards (collapsed seat), forwards (hollow seat), or to one side (collapsed hip).

- **Hip joints.** These should be pressed slightly forward, with the pelvis upright so that the side seams of the breeches are upright and at right angles to the horse's back.

- **Legs.** The thighs should be flat on the saddle. The muscles should have minimal tone and tension in the thigh, hip joint, or anywhere in the leg. The knee points to the front, as does the toe, helping the rider to sit deeper in the saddle. The knee joint should not be forced into the saddle but should be relaxed so that the lower leg hangs down, lying softly on the horse's side. The legs should have the tone to maintain a constant contact with the horse's sides.

- **Feet.** The widest part of the foot rests on the stirrup iron with only sufficient weight to retain the iron. The stirrup irons should be level, with no extra weight on the inside or outside of the foot, the heel slightly lower than the toe with the ankle joint remaining supple.

- **Arms and hands.** The upper arm should be relaxed, hanging down and not behind the vertical. The shoulders and elbow joints should be flexible to allow the hands to follow the movements of the horse's head. There should be a minimum of tension in the forearm and in the hand and there should be a straight line from the elbow, through the hand to the horse's mouth. Looking from above, the straight line will run from the outside of the forearm, through the back of the hand, down the rein, to the horse's mouth. The thumb should be uppermost. The reins are held at the base of the fingers and come out over the top of the hand, where the thumb rests lightly on them (see also page 94). The fingers should be closed but not clenched, so that if the rider were holding a bird in each hand, the bird would be allowed to breathe but not to fly away.

Outline from the rear

Viewed from the rear (see below) a straight line would run through the middle of the rider's head, down the spine, through the centre of the back of the saddle and the horse's spine. On turns and circles the angle of the rider's body should stay exactly in line with the angle of the horse's body in relation to the ground: i.e. suppleness should allow the rider to move with the horse's movement and follow his direction (see below right).

The rider's position viewed from the rear.

Position of horse and rider viewed from above.

rider sitting symmetrically

rider with collapsed right hip

on a straight line

turning to the right

- **Head.** The head and neck must be square on the shoulders and not tilted to either side.

- **Shoulders.** The shoulders should be at equal height without hunching or stiffness.

- **Elbows.** The elbows should be level with one another, not stretched away from the body or glued to the sides, and should hang naturally.

- **Seat.** The hip joints should be square to the front, with the weight resting evenly on both seat bones, the central seam of the breeches being in line with the centre of the saddle.

- **Lower legs.** The lower legs should be level with one another. They should hang down, not stretched, from the horse's sides and with the inside of the lower legs quietly in contact with the horse's sides.

- **Feet.** The feet should be level, and should have equal weight on both stirrup irons without having more weight on the inside or outside of the irons. The ankles should be at equal angles.

The seat

To use the seat correctly when riding it helps to understand its anatomy and methods of movement.

At the upper ends of the thighs (femurs) are the balls of the ball-and-sockets of the hip* joints. The sockets of the right and left hip joints are about one-third the way up the right and left hip bones (each hip bone consists of the ilium above, the ischium below and behind, and the pubis below and in front – see illustration). The two hip bones form the front, sides and part of the back of the pelvis which is an oval-shaped (in horizontal section), almost rigid girdle. The lowest points of the pelvis are the seat bones. The ridges of bone at the front of the pelvis which can be

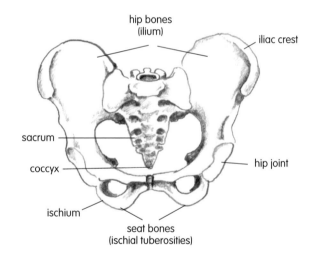

The pelvic girdle.

---

* The term 'hip' tends to be used loosely and may refer to the hip joints or the hip bones, or the iliac crests, or the medical definition of the ischium, ilium and pubis. In this book, to avoid confusion, the medical definition for the hips is used.

felt just below the waist are the iliac crests. The lower forward points of the pelvis which can be felt at the bottom of the abdomen are right and left pubic bones. At the back, the ring of the pelvic girdle is completed by the sacrum. This consists of fused rigid vertebrae which articulate with the lumbar vertebrae which run from just above to just below the waist. They are mobile, and above them the thoracic vertebrae are more rigid. On either side of the lumbar vertebrae are the loins, which are the sections of the body on both sides of the spine lying between the hip bones and the false ribs. These are the ribs that are not attached to the breastbone.

The rider's seat can move because:

- The lumbar spine is mobile.

- The pelvis can be tipped. From the pivot of where the rigid sacrum (rear section of the pelvis) and the mobile lumbar vertebrae are connected the pelvis can be tipped forwards (iliac crests forward, pubic bones backward), and backwards, largely through use of the abdominal and back muscles.

- The hip joints enable the thighs and seat to move independently of each other.

The pelvis can also be:

- Tipped sideways (by bending the lumbar vertebrae) when one hip joint is lowered and moves sideways to result in a collapsed hip.

- Turned so that in relation to the trunk this will result in one seat bone moving forward and round and the other backward in the opposite direction.

Common mistakes and why they happen

Tipping forward

This is when the rider's head and shoulders incline forward and their weight is transferred from the seat bones onto the pubic arch. As a result the position of the lower leg is weakened and it is liable to slide too far back, causing tightness in the inner thigh and a tendency to grip with the knee in a forlorn hope that this will stabilise the position. This is perhaps the most common fault that we see in beginner riders who have yet to develop the balance and strength in their posture. When under stress, such as the new experience of riding a horse, most people revert to the foetal position, which makes them curl up and crouch towards the horse's neck and withers. Only when they have developed sufficient core stability, which comes with development of the abdominal muscles, will they be able to maintain a balanced and stable position. Gentle controlled work without stirrups, such as on the lunge, is frequently the quickest way to build up these muscles.

Another factor which will cause this tendency is an over-reliance on the reins for security. As a result any change in the horse's own balance, causing him to readjust by moving his head down and forward, will cause the rider to be pulled forward and off their seat bones. The horse's own conformation and level of schooling could also have an effect, as the horse's natural balance as a grazing animal is to carry 60 per cent of his weight over his forelegs, and this is even more exaggerated when riding a young or uneducated horse who as yet has not adjusted to the weight of the rider. So horses who work on the forehand and as a result become strong in the rein contact are not the ideal mounts for the beginner rider.

Sitting behind the movement

This is less common than tipping forward, but tends to happen more in male riders, for obvious reasons related to the male conformation! As a consequence the rider's weight is transferred towards the back of the saddle, the cantle, and the weakest part of the horse's spine, the loins. This in turn throws the rider's lower leg too far forward and therefore renders it ineffective. A secondary result is that the reins will become too long and the rider will struggle to maintain an elastic contact with the horse's mouth. Other

Common mistakes and why they happen.

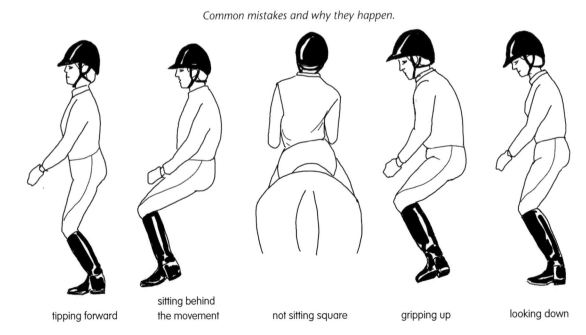

tipping forward   sitting behind   not sitting square   gripping up   looking down
                         the movement

possible causes could be a poorly fitting saddle that does not sit square on the horse's back and as a result gives the rider the feeling that the centre of balance is too far back. Sometimes, fitting a back raiser pad to lift the cantle of the saddle and readjust the balance can rectify this, but in other cases changing the saddle may be necessary – and it is usually the preferred option. Riders who constantly allow the reins to slip and become too long often develop a leaning back strategy to compensate in their attempts to maintain the contact. Using a pair of reins with grips or markers may help enhance the rider's awareness of this problem.

Not sitting square

Unfortunately for the horse this is one of the more common rider faults and is often one of the most difficult to feel and correct. Very few of us are symmetrical in our own conformation and frequently we have one leg longer than the other; this results in a tendency to overload one side of our torso and put more weight down into one stirrup iron. If we ride the same horse over a period of months then he will gradually change his own muscular development in order to compensate, and this in turn could lead to long-term chronic unsoundness. The quickest and most effective way to correct this is to ride frequently without stirrups, as the brain's natural gyro will override the rider's poor muscle memory and centralise the torso.

Another common cause can be a saddle that has a twisted tree and as a result does not sit square on the horse's back; this can also lead to uneven distribution of flocking in the panel of the saddle, which will have an adverse effect on the rider's lateral balance. Occasionally a rider who was previously straight but has become tipped to one side can be indicative of a hind leg lameness developing in the horse as the animal seeks to move the rider's weight across and over the sound leg.

Gripping up

This also results in the rider drawing up into a more foetal position as the rider applies the misconception that they will stay with the horse if they tighten their grip through the inside of their thighs and around the horse's ribs with their lower legs. As a consequence the leg is effectively shortened and the heel drawn up and back and the whole position is rendered very unstable. This position is frequently a result of a lack of confidence in the rider and progress at this stage must be slow and gentle until more trust is developed and the rider recognises that they can stay secure from balance rather than grip. Owing to the collapsing of the diaphragm the rider will quickly become breathless and this will also inhibit their coordination. Again, short periods without the stirrups will help to build up the muscles required, and enable the rider to recognise the feel of the seat being in the centre of the saddle and providing a more secure balance, and more poise through the torso.

Looking down

Many riders feel that by watching the horse's head and neck they are developing a better feel for how the horse is performing, and that this helps them to gauge what the horse is thinking next. To a certain extent this is true as the horse's ears are his early warning system, and the rider will know that all is well when they see the ears flicking gently back and forth listening to the rider's aids. However, as described earlier, this movement of the head forward, no matter how slight, can have an adverse effect on the overall balance and the rider must be encouraged to look without moving their head excessively, and to learn to feel the horse's movement through their seat. This can be done by riding for a few steps, in a safe environment, with their eyes closed, as this will enhance their other senses and increase their sense of feel.

Other influences that could affect the rider's position and balance

Conformation of the rider

As mentioned earlier, the general shape of the rider will have an overall effect on their ability to balance and stay secure. The ectomorphic person who is tall and slim in the muscles and legs with low fat storage will generally find dressage easier as they can use the length in their leg to gain greater stability and this can result in an ability to be softer with their seat, allowing for more harmony with their horse. Needless to say the differences in the conformation of the genders will also have an effect. A rather well-endowed woman may well struggle with her upper body balance and will require greater core stability to avoid being pulled forward by the horse.

Fitness and confidence of the rider

It is a widespread misconception that riding is an easy sport as the horse does most of the work. Research has shown, however, that for the beginner/novice rider it is the third most energetic sport after Nordic skiing and swimming in the sea, as it requires the greatest use of all the body's muscles and burns the most calories. It is important to recognise when the rider is suffering from fatigue as this will lead to a loss of coordination and a lack of judgement, which may result in dire consequences. This will lead to an adverse effect on the confidence of the rider, resulting in their brain being able to exert a strong negative effect over their body and their muscles' ability to function correctly.

Problems with everyday footwear

This issue generally applies only to women! Riders trying the sport for the first time as adults may experience some difficulty if they have spent much of their life wearing high-heeled shoes, as this has the effect of encouraging their Achilles tendons to shorten, making it difficult to maintain the straight line hip to heel, with the heel slightly lowered, in their early stages of learning. Work on the ground, before mounting, gently stretching and flexing the muscles and tendons downward over the edge of a step is the easiest way to alleviate this problem.

Handed dominance

In order to maintain an even development in the suppleness and muscles of the horse it is necessary for the rider to be as close to ambidextrous as possible. As most of the population tends to favour using their right-hand side this can lead to difficulties concerning the application of the aids, as they will be inclined to be stronger with their right leg and subconsciously more inclined to use the right rein, resulting in an uneven contact with the horse's mouth. Overdevelopment of the muscles on the right-hand side will result in an uneven weight balance, which could encourage crookedness.

Conformation of the horse

As balance is the key to a correct and effective position the shape of the horse and therefore his ability to carry his own weight and that of the rider equally over all four legs is going to be affected by the make and shape of the horse. A horse with an over-large head and a strong forehand is going to balance more strongly over the forelegs and may leave the rider constantly pulled forward over the horse's withers as the horse strives to use the rider as a 'fifth leg'. The rider must strive to stay in the centre of balance and not let the horse take charge of their position.

Design and style of the saddle used

Not only is it essential that the saddle fits the horse; it must also be the right size for the rider and suit the style of riding that is to be undertaken. The average adult will need a saddle that is either 17½ or 18 inches in length from pommel to cantle, in order to sit in balance with comfort. When starting, a general-purpose saddle is ideal as it is not too structured so as to force the rider into a more extreme position that their muscles are not yet ready to accommodate.

Terrain ridden over and the speed of riding

When learning, it is likely that the rider will ride on the flat surface of an arena. However, one of the greatest experiences can be to ride out in the countryside over uneven terrain in a variety of gaits. This will lead to the horse making multiple changes in his natural balance and as a result the rider will constantly be aware of having to shift position in order to maintain a stable posture. This is best done by shortening the stirrup leathers two to three holes in order that the rider's weight may be easily shifted from the seat to down the back of the legs and onto the stirrup irons, thus enabling the rider to develop more stability.

Medical conditions

Riders must be well aware of any previous or existing medical conditions that would hamper their ability to perform. For example, an old back injury may limit their suppleness and have an effect on their capability to follow the movement on a big-moving horse. An asthmatic may suffer with shortness of breath and as a result may have to limit long periods of sustained work.

Riders who, for whatever reason, take medication may need to be aware that this can have a dulling effect on the senses and may well limit muscle function and coordination, making body awareness more difficult. Instructors should be informed in such cases.

Stress

This may be caused by competing, or other external factors. Sports research has shown that, in moments of stress, the quality of performance can drop by a third, and when experiencing extreme duress a mere 3 per cent of our brain is available to us. Therefore, especially in competitions, it is essential that the quality of a rider's position is well rehearsed and that it requires little conscious effort to sustain it.

Changes required in balance for faster work and jumping

When riding over uneven terrain, especially if there are going to be fairly frequent periods of canter or even gallop, or when jumping fences, the balance of the horse will shift more forward, with the centre of gravity moving more over the forelegs. In order to accommodate this, the rider should shorten their stirrup leathers and close all the angles in the joints from the hips down. This will incline the shoulders forward and the natural straight line will become ear, shoulder, knee, toe, over the more forward centre of balance. This will enable the joints to take up the concussion and jar created by the terrain and landing over fences by using them as shock-absorbers. It would not be unusual for event riders to shorten their leathers as many as seven holes from their dressage length, in order to go cross-country.

It is important to note that, in order to stay over the horse's centre of balance, as the rider's shoulders go forward and their hands lower and move forward on each side of the horse's neck, so their hips must slide back towards the cantle of the saddle. Because it is important to avoid putting weight on the weakest part of the horse's spine (the loins), which are immediately behind the saddle, the rider should transfer more weight onto the stirrup irons and lighten the weight that goes through the seat. This is sometimes known as a two-point position. As a result the stability of the position is reliant on a strong and secure lower leg that stays close to or just behind the girth. Tightening and gripping through the knee will result in the lower leg being inclined to swing back, resulting in the rider tipping forward and collapsing on the horse's neck.

As the horse needs freedom of the head and neck to change and stabilise his balance the rider must ensure that they have the physical muscular strength to sustain the position without reliance on the reins or collapsing back onto the seat. This will require further development of the core muscles as well as the quadriceps down the front of the thigh, and those muscles running down the back of the calf. To promote this riders should be prepared to practise as much time riding on short stirrup leathers and in two-point position as they would expect to practise without stirrups, in order to develop their basic position for work on the flat.

Postural adaptations for jumping, and jumping technique are discussed further in Chapter 5. See also Chapter 18 for information on cross-country jumping.

3. Early Lessons

HAVING CHOSEN A RIDING SCHOOL and felt confident about the initial contact made with the centre, the rider should have been advised about what to wear for the first lesson and whether or not a hat can be hired from the school. On arrival, there should be a clear procedure: either the client will be met by the instructor, or will go to the reception or office, to be advised who the instructor will be and the name of the horse being ridden.

The very basics of starting to ride have been discussed in Chapter 1. Following on from these, the first few lessons should follow a standard format. In addition to activities such as leading in hand, mounting and dismounting, instruction should be given in how to check the girth, how to run down the stirrups, and how to put the reins over the horse's head. All these activities should be closely monitored and assistance readily offered by the instructor.

Instruction may be in a small group of riders (two to four) of the same standard, or it may be on a one-to-one basis. Private lessons obviously cost more than group lessons.

Beginner riders may be led by a junior member of staff, with one instructor in charge of the actual teaching. Riders may learn on a lead rein or on the lunge – the differences are discussed in greater detail later in the book.

Tightening the girth whilst in the saddle.

Adjusting the stirrups whilst in the saddle. Throughout, the rider keeps both feet in the stirrups for security.

The first few lessons should cover the correct method for preparing to mount the horse, mounting, and of course, dismounting. The basic riding position will be demonstrated, and the rider will be encouraged to try to adopt this at halt before experiencing any movement of the horse.

Picking up the reins, learning how to hold them and how to lengthen and shorten them should be an essential part of the first lesson. Often, however, there will be times in the early sessions when the rider is asked to hold the pommel of the saddle or a neck strap to help balance and security. Riders will also be shown how to tighten the girth and adjust the stirrups from the saddle.

The rider's first experience of the horse's movement should be in walk, and the rider should be introduced to the concept of transitions up and down, with the accompanying information on the use and coordination of legs and hands to give aids, or messages, to the horse. If the rider is confident and showing no signs of worry or nervousness trot will usually be tried in the first or second lesson.

The duration of lessons for novice riders will usually be 30 or 40 minutes maximum. Fitness and ability to concentrate must be the governing factors here, especially at first.

The beginner rider should endeavour to ride at least once a week so that continuity is achieved through reasonably frequent repetition. However, progress will depend on many factors in addition to lesson frequency. Enjoyment and satisfaction must be paramount as well as an overall sense of achievement. This does not mean that every session will result in a burgeoning feeling of success. The general feeling over several lessons, however, must be one of pleasure and progress, even if some of the components of the sessions are difficult or challenging for the rider.

Riding school terms

Leading in hand – lead your horse, usually to the area where you will ride and/or back to his stable.

Run down the stirrups – to pull the stirrup irons down the stirrup leathers, ready for use.

Run up the stirrups – to slide the stirrup irons up to the top of the leathers so that they are safe when leading the horse.

'Go large' – ride around the perimeter of the arena/school using the outside track.

'On the right rein' – moving in a clockwise direction.

'On the left rein' – moving in an anticlockwise direction.

'Change the rein' – make a change of direction from the left rein to the right rein, or vice versa, within the school.

'Inner track' – the inside track, about 1.5m/5ft inside the outer track; usually regarded as allowing room for one horse to pass comfortably on the outside track.

'Pass left to left' – when riding in a school or arena riders traditionally pass left shoulder (or hand) to left shoulder (hand), unless otherwise instructed.

'Take the reins over the head' – both reins are taken over the horse's head, usually to enable the (unmounted) rider to lead the horse in hand.

'Quarter markers' – the arena letters F, H, K and M.

'Half markers' – the arena letters B and E.

'Centre line' – an imaginary line between A and C, the centre of which is X.

'Leading file' – the rider at the front of a line of (single file) riders.

'Rear file' – the rider at the back of a line of (single file) riders.

'Whole ride…' – means all the riders together.

'In succession…' – means one rider at a time.

'Prepare to…' – a term that informs the rider of the need to get ready to give an aid or sequence of aids to tell the horse what to do next.

'Track left' – turn left on reaching the track.

'Track right' – turn right on reaching the track.

'Make much of your horse/pony' – give your horse/pony a pat as a reward.

'Near-side' – the left side of the horse.

'Off-side' – the right side of the horse.

Making progress

So, during the first half dozen lessons the beginner rider can expect to cover the following basic riding skills:

- Mounting and dismounting.
- The basic riding position.
- Picking up the reins and holding them.
- Shortening and lengthening the reins.
- The aids for moving forward to walk from halt and from walk to halt.
- The concept of transitions from one gait to another.
- How to turn the horse left and right.
- Developing the walk gait into trot.
- Understanding the difference between rising and sitting trot.
- Establishing rhythm and coordination in rising trot.
- Developing balance and coordination in walk and trot.
- Basic school figures and terms relating to 'going large' around the school.
- Riding turns, inclines and circles.
- Understanding the need to work evenly on both reins.
- Making changes of rein.
- Appreciating the value of working without stirrups and gradually developing this work.
- Working with increasing independence from the leader or lunger.
- Taking greater responsibility, as balance improves, for controlling the horse.
- Establishing a more independent riding position.

The ability to control the horse (in a novice lesson) without assistance from the ground may be achieved in six lessons, but for some riders it may take longer.

The most import criteria in these early lessons are that:

- The lessons are enjoyable and constructive.

- The tuition is clear and the rider feels confident to question anything about which there is any uncertainty.

- The rider feels positive and enthusiastic to try again after the lesson.

- The rider should become aware that riding is a partnership and should be encouraged to communicate with the horse, treating him with respect and not as an inanimate object.

Position in movement in walk and trot

Walk

The horse walks in four time. The walk is a marching gait in which each of the feet is put down individually, one after the other, with no moment of suspension (i.e. when all four feet are off the ground).

He nods his head as each foreleg comes to the ground, and to keep the correct rein contact the rider's hands must invite this movement and not restrict it. The fingers remain closed on the reins and the correct contact is maintained. The rider remains sitting upright, but the supple seat moves to allow and not to restrict the horse's body movements. When the horse walks well there is considerable movement of his back muscles. This movement is essential if the horse is to remain supple, coordinated and free in his gaits. Therefore the rider must allow this movement to occur through supple action of the loins, but not by moving the upper back. It is usual for the pelvis to move in the rhythm of the gait. A good exercise for developing both suppleness and feel is to allow the seat bones to move alternately so that as the left hind leg is lifted forward the rider allows the left seat bone forward in accordance with the horse's muscle movement and then the right seat bone with the right hind leg. This movement in the rider's seat and loins should not be exaggerated and should be barely perceptible to an onlooker.

Trot

The horse trots in two time. His legs move in diagonal pairs: near fore and off hind, off fore and near hind. The trot can be ridden sitting or rising.

Sitting trot

The rider sits softly; the seat in contact with the saddle. The body remains upright. The movement of the horse's back is absorbed mostly through the rider's loins but also through the seat, thighs, knees and ankles. The hands keep a consistent, elastic contact. The spring of the trot is such that in absorbing the movement, the rider should feel rather as though riding the crests of small waves. Thus, the thighs feel supple and the pelvis is cushioned by the seat. As in the walk, the rider's movement must not be exaggerated, resulting in the back hollowing or the waist collapsing. Any excess tension or gripping will cause the rider to bump instead of remaining in a quiet, balanced position in contact with the saddle on the horse's back.

Rising trot

Working in time with the diagonal two-beat trot, the rider rises on one beat of the trot and sits on the next beat. It is essential that this is done in perfect balance so as not to upset the horse's rhythm. The rider's body is inclined slightly forward from the pelvis with the pelvis tipped forward; the rider should sit softly without allowing the weight to go backwards. The shoulders and elbows allow the hands to go with the movement of the horse's head and neck, which, in the trot, hardly move.

Rising trot on a named diagonal

Learning to ride on a particular diagonal is achieved gradually. It is helpful at first to watch the horse's shoulders moving backwards and forwards in the walk. The rider needs to be able to glance down at the shoulder whilst riding the horse forward in the usual way. As the shoulder moves forward, the forefoot is off the ground, and as the shoulder moves back, the forefoot is taking weight on the ground. Watching in walk will give the rider the idea of what to look for in trot, when the shoulder action is that much quicker.

To attempt this in trot, the rider should start off in sitting trot, and then establish rising trot. When the trot is forward and in a good rhythm, and only then, the rider should start to glance at the horse's shoulders (each one in turn) and try to decide which shoulder is coming back during the 'sitting' phase. If the right shoulder is coming back, then the rider is sitting as the diagonal pair of right forefoot and left hind foot meet the ground (this is called the right diagonal – named from the foreleg). If the rider is sitting as the left shoulder is moving back, the left forefoot is on the ground and the rider is on the left diagonal.

Gradually the rider will become more adept at recognising the diagonal and can then try changing from one diagonal to the other. This is achieved by sitting for an extra beat or 'bounce' in the saddle, which causes the rider to 'come up' on the other diagonal.

Rising on the correct (in this case, left) diagonal.

the rider's seat comes out of the saddle as the horse's left shoulder goes forward

the rider's seat returns to the saddle as the horse's left shoulder comes back

Learning to sit for an extra beat takes practice. Changing diagonal in rising trot enables the rider to remain in good balance and prevents the horse from becoming 'one-sided'. It also improves the rider's coordination and will, in time, enable the development of 'feel' in the rider.

Learning to ride on the lunge or lead rein

There are advantages and disadvantages in both of these very viable means of teaching the beginner rider. Each will be considered on its merits. Ultimately, each rider must decide on their own preferred method (assuming that both are on offer) and then discuss the issues with the riding school.

Learning on the lunge

- The horse must be safe and experienced as a lunge horse for beginners. He must be calm and obedient.

- The horse's trot should be neither too big nor bouncy, which a novice rider would find difficult to cope with or sit to.

- The instructor must be competent in lungeing the horse well and teaching the novice simultaneously. This arguably requires greater skill than giving a lead-rein lesson.

- The physical demands made on a lunge horse are greater than those made on a lead-rein horse.

- Lungeing requires a one-instructor-to-one-pupil ratio, so is labour intensive.

- Lungeing requires a minimum area of 20m x 20m for the lesson. It is advisable for the area to be enclosed, and with sound footing.

- One horse should not be expected to repeat several lunge lessons daily, nor be lunged on every working day because of the physical effort involved.

- Some novice riders feel insecure when on the end of a lunge rein, well away from the instructor's direct control.

- Some novice riders prefer the greater feeling of independence that the lunge gives them over the lead rein.

- There are limitations in the visibility that the lunger/teacher has of the pupil. Some faults in straightness or position of the outside of the rider may go unnoticed.

- Lungeing can be valuable for developing the position, effect and feel of any level of rider, from novice to advanced.

Learning on a lead rein

- Often more suitable for children and ponies; a number of riders can be taught by one instructor while being led by competent leaders.

- The horse or pony can cope with a number of sessions in one day as being led is far less physically intensive than being lunged.

- Some nervous riders feel more secure and confident in having someone in control of the horse close by.

- In groups, novice riders often gain support and encouragement from each other.

- Some adult riders feel rather belittled by being led.

- The pony/horse must be calm, good tempered, easy to lead in walk and trot on both reins, and comfortable.

- Some beginners may be offered one or two lessons on the lead rein before progressing to the lunge.

After the initial lunge or lead-rein lessons the beginner rider should progress to riding unattended when the following have been achieved:

- Basic balance and coordination in walk and trot, independent of the reins.

- Basic understanding of the aids to stop, start and turn.

- A level of basic competence that will allow further development of skills behind a competent leading file.

4. Improving on the Lunge

ONE OF THE BEST WAYS OF ESTABLISHING THE CORRECT POSITION in the saddle and improving a rider's balance is to ride without stirrups both on and off the lunge. The main advantage of riding on the lunge is that the rider can leave the control of the horse to another, and can concentrate on position. However, this will only be achieved if the rider has complete confidence in the person doing the lungeing and if the horse is suitable. (This chapter is limited to giving guidance on how to establish a rider's basic position by riding on the lunge without stirrups. The technique of lungeing a horse without a rider differs considerably and is dealt with in Chapter 10, which also covers in more detail the facilities and tack required for lungeing.)

There will come a time when the novice rider will wish to dispense with the lunge and to start riding, using reins and stirrups, and controlling the horse. This is acceptable once the rider has acquired a stable seat, and is the next step in a rider's education. The means by which control is exercised are discussed in Chapters 5–7.

But even after the beginner has dispensed with the lunge and can control the horse without such assistance, riding without stirrups is still a most useful way of developing the correct position in the saddle. Many advanced riders do much work without stirrups, finding that they are more in harmony with their horse and so more effective.

Lungeing a rider of any level is always helpful as it allows the rider to work on position, suppleness, balance and feel.

Responsibilities of the instructor

Instructing the rider on the lunge

Anyone undertaking the lungeing of a rider should be well versed in lungeing and sufficiently knowledgeable to be able to correct the rider's position and assist in its being maintained at all gaits. The instructor is responsible for modifying the horse's gaits and transitions to suit the rider. Sometimes it may be helpful to use an assistant to lead the horse and give confidence to or support a novice in the first stages of riding on the lunge.

The rider's safety

When lungeing a rider, the instructor is entirely responsible for the pupil's safety and must do everything possible to avoid anything untoward happening which could reduce the rider's confidence. Only if a rider can work without tension will work on the lunge be of value. An instructor should pay attention to the following points, all of which have a bearing on the horse's and rider's safety:

- Lungeing should be carried out in a satisfactory environment.

- Tack should be strong and well fitted.

- The lunge horse should be suitable.

- Lessons should not be too long and must contain rest periods.

- Instructor, rider and horse should be correctly turned out. The instructor should always wear gloves when handling a lungeing rein, and should remove spurs, if worn. The rider should wear breeches and boots or jodhpurs and must wear a hard hat conforming to current safety standards.

Facilities needed

The lungeing area

Lungeing should always be carried out in a reasonably quiet place so that neither the horse's nor the rider's attention is distracted and the instructor's commands can be clearly heard by both. The going must be good. The whole area should be level and, if possible, should be enclosed as this will greatly increase a novice rider's confidence and help the horse's concentration. It follows that an indoor riding school is often an ideal site for a lesson but it is certainly not essential.

An outdoor area can be marked off by use of straw bales, poles and jump stands or the like.

Tack

The tack needed when lungeing a horse and rider consists of:

- A snaffle bridle. The reins should be twisted around under the neck and the throatlash put through one of the loops (see illustration, page 129), when working-in prior to mounting the rider. Knot the reins on the horse's neck once the rider is mounted so that the rider can pick them up in an emergency.

- A cavesson. This is fitted over or under the bridle and buckled under the chin like a drop noseband, or above the bit like cavesson noseband, with the lunge rein fastened to the central swivel ring on the noseband. The noseband and cheek strap must be tightened sufficiently to prevent them pulling round or rubbing the horse's outside eye.

- A lunge rein. About 10m (33ft) long, made of linen webbing or nylon, with a large loop at one end and a swivel joint, attached to a buckle or spring clip, at the other.

- Side-reins should be used with caution and only fastened to the bit after the pupil has mounted, and removed before the pupil dismounts. They should run horizontally from the girth about halfway up the horse's sides to his mouth. (For the correct length see page 133.) When not in use they should be clipped to the Ds of the saddle.

- A saddle (a dressage model, preferably). It is important for the saddle to fit both horse and rider. The use of a numnah is recommended.

- A lunge whip.

- Brushing boots for all four legs.

The lunge horse

Ideally, the horse to be used by a rider on the lunge should be a specialist at the job, but a lunge horse must do other work if he is not to become thoroughly stale. Temperament is very important and he must be obedient to the human voice – since, on the lunge, this will be the principal aid. The gaits should be comfortable. Circling is a strain on a horse and a fit and mature animal of 6 years or over should be used. The time spent on the lunge should not exceed 20 minutes (excluding rest periods) if the horse is being used actively.

Technique for lungeing a rider

The instructor

The instructor stands in the centre of the lungeing circle, which ideally should be between 15m and 20m in size, and drives the horse around the circle, holding the lunge

Training on the lunge.

The depth of the seat and the rider's feel can be improved by selective work without stirrups and/or reins. Here the rider's stirrups are safely crossed in front of the saddle, the reins are secured by a knot, and the rider has one hand on the pommel of the saddle.

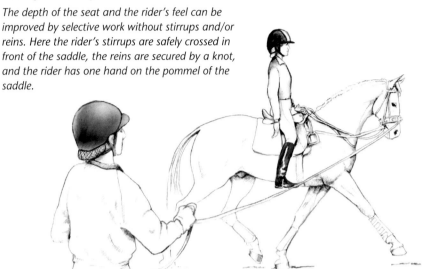

rein in the hand towards which the horse is moving, and holding the whip in the other hand. Instructors can hold the loop at the end of the lunge rein in either hand. The instructor must concentrate on the rider and on the horse's hindquarters rather than on his forehand. It is important to ensure that the horse describes a true circle; and the instructor should endeavour to stand fairly still, which should be possible if the horse is active and obedient. A trained lunge horse should be obedient to the instructor's voice. The lunge whip should seldom have to be used, but when it is needed the horse should be touched lightly and usually above the hind fetlocks. Whenever the instructor moves closer to the horse, the whip should be reversed, with the thong trailing to the rear.

Length of a lungeing lesson

As already mentioned, a horse being used actively should not be lunged for more than some 20 minutes, excluding rest periods. Frequent rest periods will be needed, since riding without stirrups can be tiring for riders. The horse should be worked equally on each rein.

Preliminary work

Before the start of a lesson, an instructor will often wish to begin by lungeing the horse without a rider, to loosen him up and make sure he is calm and obedient. Many riders like to 'warm up' by riding on the lunge but using their stirrups. Both measures may be used with advantage.

The lunge lesson

Rider position

The person lungeing and instructing must ensure that the rider takes up and maintains the correct position in the saddle as defined in Chapter 2. The rider, with the horse stationary, sits in the deepest part of the saddle, with the weight on the seat bones and the legs hanging loosely down against the saddle. To achieve this position, the rider should take hold of the front of the saddle with both hands and gently pull the seat into the lowest part, making the upper body as upright as possible, so that a vertical line running from the ear through the point of the shoulder bisects the hip joint and touches the back of the heel. (The side-reins should not be attached until work on the move begins.)

The following two points should be particularly noted:

- There should be no deviation from the line: ear-shoulder-hip-heel. A rider sitting in a fork seat will tend to be in front of the vertical line; a rider whose weight is transferred from seat bones to buttocks will tend to be behind this line. (See illustrations on pages 36-37.)

- The inner thigh muscles must be relaxed so that the knee lies sufficiently low on the saddle to enable the rider gradually to gain more security in the correct position.

Exercise to assist in achieving the correct position

The following simple and short exercise may be carried out before starting work, either when halted or at walk. The movements should never be jerky and the timing must be left to the rider, the exercise being repeated two or three times. The rider, holding the front of the saddle, stretches both legs sideways away from the horse's sides, then allows the legs to relax completely and to fall gently back on to the saddle, the knee being as low as possible, without straining.

Exercise to build confidence

At all three gaits and on both reins the rider can take one hand off the saddle and allow this arm to hang down just behind the thigh on the same side for a circle or two. The whole arm should be relaxed, as this exercise should begin to instil in the rider the importance of a relaxed upper arm once holding the reins. When the rider can let go of the saddle, both arms may be dropped together, care being taken that the waist does not collapse or the shoulders become rounded.

Work at the walk

Lungeing the rider at the walk can be used to give confidence to beginners or nervous riders. There is very little upward thrust in the movement of the horse's back, but an active walk will displace the rider's balance on a horizontal and slightly diagonal plane and riders must be taught that this motion must be absorbed through the suppleness of their loins and seat and must not result in a rocking action of the upper body.

Although all exercises that follow can be carried out at the walk, for more experienced riders the walk is best used for checking the rider's position and during rest periods when the rider is allowed to sit at ease.

If much work is being carried out in walk, it is essential that the side-reins are long enough not to cause restriction to the normal free movement required by the horse's head and neck in walk.

Sitting to the trot on the lunge

Once in the correct position at the walk and with the rider still holding the saddle if required, the horse can be sent quietly forward into a trot, as long as the speed, action and spring of the gait are well within the rider's capabilities. Advanced riders will be able to cope with more activity and scope in the trot than will novice riders. The rider should concentrate on maintaining their own position with tone but without gripping. Only when the seat and balance are fully established should the rider be encouraged to learn to use the seat to control the movement and action of the horse. At the sitting trot, the rider should adjust to the two-time rhythm of the trot and, remaining supple and with tone, allow the weight of the straight body to sink softly down into the saddle as each pair of diagonal legs meets the ground; horse and rider will then rebound as one during the periods of suspension. A rider who has achieved this will be able to sit still in relation to the movement of the horse.

Rising to the trot on the lunge

Rising to the trot without stirrups has little to commend it, except as a strengthening exercise for jumping and racing. Should a rider need to improve rising technique, the stirrups should therefore be re-attached and the leathers so adjusted that the rider can make and easily retain contact, with the widest part of the feet on the irons and with the heels lower than the toes. It is important to adapt the length of leather to suit the rider's position and not the other way round. If the leathers are too short, either tension will develop – especially in the knees and ankles – or, more likely, the rider's seat will move back in the saddle. If the leathers are too long, the rider's toes will constantly be dropping in an effort to make contact with the irons, so weakening the whole position.

Once the stirrup leathers are the correct length and the horse is moving in a soft, springy trot, the rider should allow this action gently to lift the seat bones from the saddle on every diagonal stride. To compensate for this movement the body should also go slightly forward from the top of the hip bones. Retaining this position the rider then sinks softly back into the saddle on the next stride. The feeling should be of 'going forward and down and not up in the air and back' (de Nemethy). The whole movement should be initiated by the action of the horse and not by the rider.

Changing the diagonal

When rising to the trot on the lunge the rider should rise as the horse's outside shoulder goes forward, thus returning to the saddle as that leg and the inside hind leg hit the ground. This is known as rising on, or using, the outside diagonal, which not only makes it easier for the horse to maintain his balance on the circle but also prevents one-sided muscular development. It also has an important part to play in the use of the aids once the horse is off the lunge. Riders should be encouraged constantly to change the diagonal by sitting down for one additional stride before rising again until they can tell instinctively which diagonal they are using.

Cantering on the lunge

The difficulties entailed when riding at a canter on the lunge are greater than at the walk or trot and this should never be attempted without an experienced, well-balanced, educated horse and an experienced instructor in charge, using a quiet place away from other horses and possible distractions.

Centrifugal force is more noticeable at the canter, and riders should guard against the use of grip to maintain their position. The upper body should not rock in rhythm with the changing horizontal levels of the horse's back; this should be absorbed through supple loins and seat. Not all exercises can be carried out at the canter, and the suitable ones are mentioned in the following paragraphs.

Canter work on the lunge with a rider is extremely demanding, physically, on the horse and therefore its use should be limited.

Mounted exercises on the lunge

When a rider has the confidence and ability to let go of the saddle and to ride easily whilst maintaining the correct position without gripping, for about 5 minutes on each rein, further mounted exercises should be attempted. These are designed to improve the rider's position, suppleness and balance and, in the case of the novice, to increase confidence.

The following general points apply to all exercises on the lunge whether at the walk, trot or canter, and should be observed by the rider and the person doing the lungeing or supervising the exercise:

- As the basis of riding is rhythm, all exercises should be carried out rhythmically in time with the horse.

- The exercises should develop balance, suppleness and strength without producing tension anywhere.

- The movement of one part of the body should not be reflected in another part.

- Breathing should be deep and controlled with a slight emphasis on exhalation, as this helps relaxation. No exercise in the saddle should make the pupil out of breath.

- All exercises should be carried out on both reins. Few riders sit in an identical position on each side and most have a tendency to twist in the saddle, causing one leg to move forward and the other slightly back.

- Twenty minutes excluding rest periods should be the maximum for work on the lunge for any but the most experienced riders.

The following exercises are suitable for riders on the lunge:

- **Correcting the position.** The rider holds the front of the saddle, keeping the seat firmly in the saddle and straightening the upper body upwards at the same time as pulling gently down into the saddle and stretching down with both legs, i.e. there should be an upward and downward correction. This should be done immediately prior to transitions and is a useful exercise at other times. Later the muscle influence of these movements is used to warn the horse that something is about to be asked of him and to ensure that the rider is in the correct position to apply the aids. The rider should develop the habit of correcting position before asking anything of the horse.

    As the rider progresses, the same exercise may be carried out with the hands in the rein position: i.e. holding imaginary reins, great care being taken that the correct position is not lost, particularly during transitions.

- **Shoulder-shrugging exercise.** Here the object is to remove any tension from the shoulders and the base of the neck. Both shoulders are drawn up as high as possible towards the ears (taking care not to tilt the head back or stick the elbows out), and then allowed to drop back into place. They must not be lowered hesitantly or pulled down forcibly. This act should be repeated five or six times; it must be done in an easy rhythm and without setting up any tension in the back or arms.

- **Head and neck exercises.** The object is to rid the neck and jaw of tension. These exercises are a logical follow-on from the previous one.

   1. The head is allowed to turn steadily anticlockwise and then clockwise. Care should be taken that the head does not tilt.

   2. Without raising the chin, the head is rolled steadily first to one side and then the other, with the ear as nearly as possible resting on the shoulders, which must not be allowed to lift.

   3. The head is allowed to roll steadily forward until the chin is resting on the chest. Care should be taken that the back does not become rounded.

      NB Exercises 1 and 3 should be performed at the halt only.

- **Arm and shoulder exercises.** The object is to flatten and stretch the muscles of the abdomen and free the shoulder joints.

   1. Steadily raise alternate arms with fingers stretched and the elbow joint straight until the arm reaches maximum height with the elbow joint beside the ear, palm facing forward.

   2. Circle the arms slowly to the rear three or four times before returning to normal position. The exercise may then be carried out with both arms simultaneously. The swing should always be backwards and in rhythm with the horse's stride. No force should be used or effort made to complete a full backward circle.

   3. Instead of circling the arms backwards, they may be moved backwards as far as they will go without strain, keeping the arm and fingers straight. The arm is then returned to the vertical position. In both 2 and 3 the shoulder and hip joints must remain parallel.

4. Raise the arms so that they are horizontal. Turn the body from the waist alternately to the left and the right, while maintaining the arms on the horizontal and at 180° to each other. The seat must remain still. This can be done at the walk and trot.

- **Spine and hip joints.** The object of these exercises is to make the spine and hip joints supple.

    1. Arm turning. Allow the arms to hang limply down and place one hand on the horse's withers and the other over the back of the saddle. Change position by twisting from the waist without losing correct position or the rhythm of the gait. The seat must not move in the saddle nor the backward arm be taken beyond the line of the horse's spine. This exercise may be safely carried out at the halt, walk or trot, but the pupil should be competent and confident before attempting it at the canter.

    2. Jockey position. While holding the front of the saddle, draw the legs up, closing the angles of the ankles, knees and hips, and come forward with the body into the racing position. At first, maintain the position for a few strides but gradually hold for longer and longer. This can be done at the walk and trot.

    3. Scissors. Lengthen legs and while maintaining seat bones in the saddle alternately swing one leg back and the other forwards. This can be done at the walk and trot.

    4. Touching toes. Take one hand and touch the toe on the opposite side. Repeat with the other hand. This exercise should be done in halt, with the instructor at the horse's head.

- **Ankle exercise.** Turn the ankles in as full a circle as possible, firstly clockwise and then anticlockwise. This can be done at all gaits. The object of this exercise is to relax and 'soften' the ankles.

5. Cantering, Jumping and Riding Out

Rider fitness

Every rider must be reasonably fit in order to be able to maintain the correct position in the saddle, to assist the horse and to enjoy riding. It is a surprising fact that the energy consumed in riding is of the same order as that used in such obviously physically demanding sports as running or cycling, so that even a novice requires a degree of basic fitness. For the advanced and the competitive rider, such as the jockey, three-day eventer, show jumper or dressage rider, a much higher standard of physical fitness is needed.

Methods of achieving fitness

While daily riding is in itself a good way of keeping fit, it is certainly not enough to reach the standard of fitness required for competition. For this, the rider's heart and lungs must work efficiently, and the muscles of the back and legs should be in particularly good condition. The rider must be supple throughout the body, and excess fat must be avoided.

It is generally agreed that the best way to keep fit is to run regularly, although skipping, swimming and cycling are all useful aids to fitness. There are also many more mounted exercises suitable for riders of all stages; dismounted exercises and yoga, which help as well as promote suppleness and coordination. Many riders have found a study of the Alexander Technique extremely helpful in improving their riding abilities, and an increasing number of riders practise Pilates.

It is most important not to overdo physical training, which must always be progressive and should take into account the rider's age and medical condition. In special cases, medical advice should be sought before a strenuous course of training is undertaken.

Learning to canter

The horse canters in three-time. The sequence of legs is: outside hind, inside hind and outside fore in a diagonal pair, then inside fore (often referred to as the 'leading leg'). In the canter, the level of the horse's body alters from front to rear. The rider must therefore adjust to this alteration in the levelness of the horse as well as absorbing the up and down spring. The rider must absorb the bounding movement of the canter with the loins and seat and not by swinging the upper body backwards and forwards – which is a very common fault. The hip joints need to be pressed forward, the shoulders remaining on the vertical (not forward) and square to the horse's shoulders. The loins move to follow the undulating movement of the canter. The three hoof beats should be felt. The rider must retain a balanced seat, not slipping to one side of the saddle. Some riders press the hip joint corresponding to the leading leg slightly more forward than the other: i.e. if the near is leading, then the left seat bone should be forward. The rider's legs must remain long, with the inside leg beside the girth and the outside slightly further back. There must be no drawing up of either leg.

The first canter lesson is, for many, a milestone in learning to ride. When the rider has achieved confidence and some balance in rising and sitting trot, and can ride a little without stirrups, then it is time to try canter. A horse who moves smoothly into canter without running into it from an unbalanced trot will help the rider stay in balance.

The first canter would probably involve simply moving into canter in a corner (after the short side of the school), travelling down one long side of the school and returning to trot before the next corner. This will enable the rider to feel the gait and begin to deal with the increased feeling of speed and the difference in how it is necessary to sit.

The horse will be able to move more easily into canter given the aids on a corner. Sitting tall and staying relaxed, the rider should give the following aids: the inside leg is applied on the girth to maintain the forward energy; the outside leg positioned a little behind the girth to ask him to move into canter on the correct leading leg (see also pages 109–110); the inside rein asks for a little bend in the direction of the corner; and the outside rein controls the speed of the trot and regulates the amount of bend.

In the downward transition to trot, the rider should sit tall and try to follow the movement into a rising trot rhythm. As confidence and competence develop, the rider will be able to canter for longer and around the corners of the school, and will also learn how to sit into the downwards transition into trot.

Having sufficient time to learn how to master the canter is the most important criterion here, closely followed by practice and patience.

Fast work – strong canters and galloping

In due course, once the rider is confident in canter, stronger canters and eventually galloping in the open may be undertaken. This work is essential for anyone preparing to take part in cross-country competitions (see also Chapter 18).

In fast work on the flat the rider must take care that:

- The stirrups are short enough: otherwise the rider tends to stand in the stirrups and open the angle of the knee. The result is that the seat bones are not close enough to the saddle.

- The rider's body is not too far forward, i.e. the angle is not more than 45° from the vertical.

- The reins are shortened to ensure the rider's hands are well in front of the body.

- See illustration below.

The light seat/jumping position.

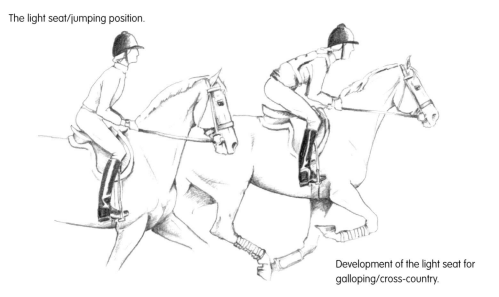

Development of the light seat for galloping/cross-country.

Learning to jump

Before learning to jump it is essential that the basic seat is well balanced and secure. This is not just to enable the rider to learn this new skill as safely as possible but also for the benefit of the horse so that he is able to jump comfortably and confidently.

The balanced jumping seat

The same basic principles apply to both riding on the flat and over fences. However, as mentioned in Chapter 2, when the horse is jumping the centre of balance moves forward and the rider will need to adapt their position. The purpose of the jumping seat is to give freedom to the horse's back and to enable the rider to follow all changes in the horse's balance while still being able to influence the horse.

In order to accommodate the horse's jump the stirrup leathers will need to be shorter. How much shorter will depend a little on the conformation of the rider and their normal flat riding length. Usually, for those learning to jump, two or three holes is sufficient so that the weight can be just out of the saddle. This adjustment to the rider's balance will enable them to develop what is known as 'the light seat'.

The rider will need to learn how to be effective with the shorter stirrup leathers as it will not normally be the seat which is the influencing aid, but rather the legs and bodyweight.

The rider's leg should remain firm and steady, the lower leg being by the girth and contributing a soft or strong forward influence on the horse as required. The leg should be ready to be strong if the need arises. The hip, knee and ankle joints must be flexible; the ability to stay in balance depends on the rider's ability to open and close the hip joint when necessary.

With beginners and novice riders it is beneficial if the rider can keep the upper body as still as possible during the approach, over the fence and when riding away from the fence. If the upper body can be kept an angle of about 45°, with the weight well down into the heels and a light seat, the rider need only offer the hand forward over the fence to give the horse sufficient freedom to make a good jump. The rider should be able to move the upper body forward fluently from the hips when necessary. However as the rider gains in experience the angle of the upper body can vary according to the type of fence, e.g. with drop fences the angle can be more open. Between the fences the hands should be quiet and steady so that the horse has to canter into the contact. The shoulder, elbow and wrist joints must be relaxed so that the rider's movements are not transmitted to the hands. The hands should be independent of the seat.

Over the fence the reins can be offered forward by taking the hands forward and down on either side of the neck – trying as far as possible to keep a straight line from the elbow through the rein to the bit. Sometimes beginners can find more confidence from placing the hands 'on the crest'. As in all riding the riders must look up and forward in the direction that they intend to go.

In order to strengthen this position a jumping or general-purpose saddle should be used as the knee rolls will help to keep the knees steady. The feet may be pushed slightly further into the stirrups to help the lower legs stay firm.

Strengthening the position

The three main points of contact with the horse are the seat, the knees and the heels. Different muscles are used in this position compared with the dressage seat and novice riders will lack strength and tire easily. A useful way to develop the rider's strength and balance is to practise riding in a 'two-point' position. Here the rider does not put any weight on the seat, transferring all the weight to the stirrups. This helps strengthen the effectiveness of the lower legs and establish a secure, independent position. Until a rider is able to maintain this balanced position in trot and canter they are unlikely to be able to stay in balance over a fence and will need to rely on the reins. If, during this exercise, the rider falls forward onto the horse's neck, the lower legs need to be moved up to the girth, underneath the rider, for support. If the rider falls back into the saddle, the lower legs will have shot too far forward.

The novice rider should be encouraged to hack out with jumping length stirrup leathers, taking up the two-point position up and down hill to further strengthen the leg position.

Transitions, both up and down, can also be made in the two-point position. This will test whether the rider can stay in balance and also whether the horse will go off the leg without the use of the seat. Many riders find it necessary to sit in the saddle and drive the horse into canter, for example, rather than just using the leg.

The lightness of the seat can be varied depending on what is required and this can also be practised by the novice rider. When the stride is free and open the seat should barely brush the saddle. However, when executing a tight turn the rider brings back the shoulders and the seat comes close to the saddle; this collects the horse's stride and brings the centre of balance back. The rider can practise this until the horse will shorten the stride merely in response to the rider's bodyweight, without any need for the rider to pull on the reins at all.

Positions from the stride before take-off, to the landing.

Overcoming fear

Many novice riders will be anxious about jumping. Fear can stem from many sources, for example the fear of the pain caused by falling off or simply from severe discomfort experienced when riding. These fears need to be discovered and allayed as far as possible. The fear of a fall can be helped by using sufficient explanation and direction throughout every stage of the learning process and by adhering to sound, safe teaching practice.

Fear of failure or ridicule is very significant. It is important for a teacher to remember the difficulties encountered when mastering a new skill; the teacher should always try to set achievable goals and never be sarcastic or short tempered. The teacher must be particularly careful when teaching groups that the competitive tendency of the participants is kept under control so that no one is made to feel inferior.

Variations in the light seat. The amount of weight in the seat to the lower leg varies but the principle remains the same.

'behind the movement'   'in front of the movement'

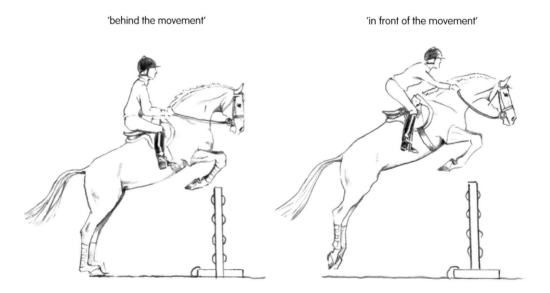

Common positional faults in jumping.

Using ground poles

Working over poles on the ground (ideally supported so they do not roll) both singly and in series is another excellent exercise. The poles can be located on a straight line (always leaving the track free) or on a curve. For trotting the ideal basic distance is 1.35m (approx 4ft 6in) but the coach must check the best distance for the individual or group of horses.

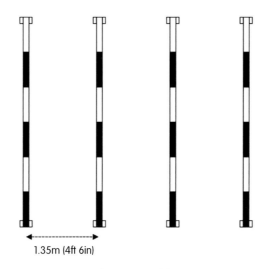

1.35m (4ft 6in)

Poles positioned for trot.

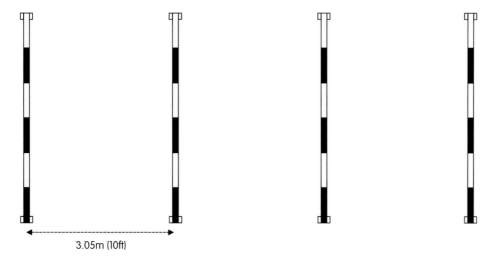

3.05m (10ft)

Poles positioned for canter.

These exercises can be carried out both in trot (initially) and canter (later) in the light seat. In each case the rider should be made aware of having a suitable rhythm and tempo to enable the horse to perform to the best of his ability.

At this stage we want the rider to intervene as little as possible on the approach to other poles.

The first jumps

Once the rider's balance is proficient over poles in the light seat, small fences can be introduced around 60cm (2ft) high, using either blocks or small wings. In trot the use of a placing pole at around 2.4–2.7m (8–9ft) will ensure the horse takes off predictably, which will help the rider to maintain the light seat and fold a little to follow the jump. Attention should be paid to the landing side to ensure that the rider remains in balance and is able to stay in control of the speed and direction. After a few lessons, canter can be introduced with the rider focusing on the rhythm of the canter. The placing pole should be removed. By this time the fence can be raised to about 76cm (2ft 6in). Counting the rhythm can be a useful tool at this stage; counting in sequences is probably most effective e.g. 1, 2, 3, 4 – 1, 2, 3, 4 and so on. Counting down 3, 2, 1 should not be encouraged as it can often lead to over-riding and over-preparation. (This counting methodology can previously have been introduced when working with ground poles.)

Jumping doubles

The rider can now be introduced to doubles. Depending on the type of horse and facilities available a second fence can be introduced to the previous set-up either as a two-stride double at 10m (33ft) or a three-stride double at 13.7m (45ft). In order to keep the rider confident and to avoid a drama should a mistake occur, it is wise for the fences to be verticals with clear ground poles. The fences for these exercises do not need to be more

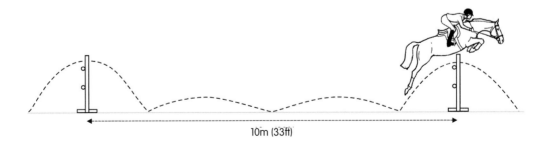

10m (33ft)

Jumping a two-stride double.

than 0.85m (2ft 9in) high and should be lower initially. The rider should be encouraged to remain in a light, balanced seat between fences, keeping rhythm and tempo in mind and simply allowing the horse to take as much rein as required without losing the contact, although to some extent this will depend on the smoothness of the horse's jumps.

The rider should be asked for feedback:

- Did the horse have to stretch for the second element?

- Did he seem to have to 'put in a short one'?

- Was the horse in the correct rhythm and tempo?

- Was the horse 'in front of the leg', in other words was he willing to go forwards?

These questions should be asked before the distance between the two fences is altered; at this stage the teacher wants the rider to get the best possible feel over the fences. The rider is not yet ready to be asked to alter the horse's approach to and through the double; that arises later in the training regime. When the rider is confident and can stay in balance throughout the approach, jump, landing and getaway, a one-stride double can be introduced. The construction and height of the fences should stay the same with a distance of 6.4m (21ft) between the two elements.

Introducing a basic course

The next logical step is to link a few fences together into a simple course. A figure-of-eight with one change of direction is sufficient at this stage. If the course is ridden in canter the rider should make smooth canter-trot-canter transitions quickly and efficiently so as to retain the horse's balance. The transitions should be ridden well before the turn and approach to the next fence. (See also Changes of lead later this chapter.) The fences should remain simple verticals with ground poles, placed so that the turns are easy and flowing to encourage the rider to keep the horse in balance.

The teacher should focus on how the rider influences the horse in between the fences. One of the finest axioms of jumping is 'look after the canter and the jump will look after itself'. The late Caroline Bradley, one of the most stylish and successful show jumpers, was heard to quote this and she practised the art of 'allowing the horse to do the jumping' to a high degree.

To reach this stage with one rider having two lessons a week will probably take about twenty lessons (maybe less if the rider is suitably competent on the flat beforehand) assuming that there are no setbacks and that the preliminary work has been completed successfully. The rider will not be perfect but will probably be ready to progress to the next stage which involves introducing different types of fences and grids.

Jumping spread fences

When introducing a spread fence it is often best to use it as the second element of a three-stride related distance. An ascending oxer is probably the easiest fence to start with and should be about 0.76m (2ft 6in) in front and 0.85m (2ft 9in) at the back, with a spread of 0.85m (2ft 9in). The front can be filled in with lower pole(s) or a dropper pole. The whole fence must be built so that it can fall if hit hard.

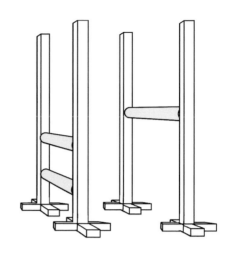

An ascending oxer is a good fence for introducing riders to jumping spreads.

When the rider is confident about the feel of a spread fence the type of fence can be varied to include a cross pole with a rail behind, and a true parallel. The height and spread should stay the same as above. The rider will now begin to feel which of these fences is the easiest to negotiate. Often the rider prefers to jump the spread fence shown in the diagram below left but care must be taken that the cross is not too high or too low. If it is too high and the horse does not stay straight he will either have to jump very big or screw sideways to clear the fence. If the cross is too low the horse may dive over the fence rather than jumping it in good style.

The rider can now be introduced to jumping a spread fence on its own, from canter. Again, the rider should be encouraged to count the rhythm; over these small training

Three types of spread fence.

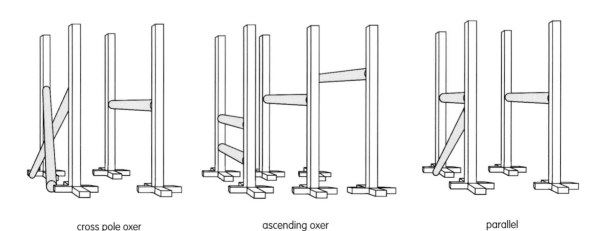

cross pole oxer   ascending oxer   parallel

fences it is not necessary for the rider to change the horse's tempo. Frequently the rider comes to the conclusion that it is easier to jump a spread than an upright and that the sensation is much more agreeable. As the rider progresses, the various types of spread fence seen in competition can be introduced in different circumstances. However, for novice riders and novice horses a spread coming out of one-stride double is not recommended, as there is less margin for error.

All of these exercises can be practised indoors or outside, on artificial surfaces or on grass. Indeed, using a variety of situations like this will now be very beneficial to the rider. If fillers are available and the horse is confident jumping them, these can occasionally be incorporated into the lesson. It is important that the fillers are not too high; a maximum height of 0.76m (2ft 6in) is sufficient. This again is to reduce the risk factor with the novice rider.

At each stage of the rider's learning process it is useful to ask the rider to ride the simple course again to check that all the main criteria are adhered to and are becoming increasingly confirmed.

Grid work

The time has now come to develop the rider's balance and coordination further by introducing grid work. Before this, however, the rider should be introduced to bounce fences. To keep the rider's confidence the exercise should start in trot and be kept small. Using a cross pole to a vertical is ideal; the rider can ride confidently to the cross pole, while having a vertical coming out gives the horse every chance to jump the fence if he is not quite straight. The exercise should start with the rider jumping a cross pole with a placing pole 2.4m (8ft) in front of it. The centre of the cross should be about 0.6m (2ft) high. The bounce jump wings should be in place about 3m (9ft 9in) from the cross pole. The rider should be encouraged to keep the horse moving forward in trot to the placing pole in order to get the feel of the horse bouncing the pole, jumping the cross pole and landing in canter. The canter should be maintained away from the fence and the horse then brought smoothly to trot. Even when jumping from trot the rider must stay in a light, balanced seat, so the rider can either stay rising or stay poised with the seat lightly brushing the saddle, but the rider must not sit in the saddle. Ideally the exercise is set up on both sides of the school so that it can be jumped on both reins. After two or three jumps in either direction the vertical can be put up at about 0.6m (2ft) so that the rider has to bounce through the exercise. The rider should be able to stay in balance and keep the horse balanced on landing.

Once the rider is confident in trot, canter can be introduced. The placing pole should be taken away and the distance between the cross pole and the vertical increased to 3.7m (12ft). The height and construction of the fences should be kept the same. The rider now knows that the horse can bounce and should be confident to present the horse to the fence in his normal, rhythmic, balanced canter.

The use of blocks or cavalletti for these exercises is not recommended because they are rather unstable and can frighten the horse if they collapse noisily in a heap. Pyramid-type Jumpkins are, however useful for grid work as they have proper plastic cups and are light and easily manoeuvrable. Using oil drums is more hazardous and best avoided.

A variety of gymnastic grids can now be used, from both trot and canter, to develop the rider's agility.

Assessing and riding a course

Measuring the distances

It is recommended that riders develop the ability to stride accurately either in 1m or 1 yd distances. Initially, riders should take three or four active strides and measure the distance that each stride covers. They will then know how much they will have to alter their natural stride in order to pace the distance between two obstacles accurately.

It is important to be able to measure distances in combinations and between individual fences accurately.

Average striding distances

Feet	Metres	Human strides	Horse strides
24	7.3	8	1
36	11	12	2
45	13.7	15	3
48	14.6	16	3
57	17.4	19	4
60	18.3	20	4

Novice riders should learn the distances for a bounce up to four non-jumping strides between fences, measured from the back of the first obstacle to the front of the next. The only exception to this is if one of the fences is a hog's back, triple bar or pheasant feeder-type fence, when the distance should be measured from the middle of the spread.

Assuming that a rider has a stride length of 0.9m (3ft) and that the average competition distance allowing one non-jumping stride between two fences is 7.3m (24ft), eight of the rider's strides would indicate an average one-stride distance. If there were only seven strides between the fences the distance would be short, while nine strides would be a long distance. An easy way to develop this measuring technique is to use the table above.

Different distances can still indicate the same number of horse's strides (as shown in the table for three and four horse strides); it is simply a matter of realising that some horses will take shorter strides than others. The implications of this for the teacher are that the rider must become aware of each individual horse's ability to lengthen or shorten his stride whilst still being able to clear the fence. The table indicates that the 'ideal' length of the horse's non-jumping stride between obstacles can vary by up to 0.9m (3ft), making a 'long' or 'short' three- or four-stride distance. His natural stride can be increased or diminished by simply shortening and lengthening the stride. However care should be taken to ensure that sufficient impulsion is kept in order to retain the balance of the horse. The rider should react with the correct body balance and rein contact; to some extent the riders have already been encouraged to do this when working over canter poles.

Another way to measure the distance between fences is to allow 1.83m (6ft) for landing and 3.7m (12ft) for each non-jumping stride between the fences. If the rider arrives at the next fence with 1.83m (6ft) to spare this will be the ideal place for the horse's take-off platform. However, the course designer may lengthen or reduce the distance between fences slightly in which case repetitions of 3.7m (12ft) distances would lead to the horse arriving too close to, or too far away from, the next fence.

Whichever method of assessing distances is used, the important aspect is for the riders to know how many strides they want their horses to take in any given situation.

Changes of lead

Before the riders attempt to jump a course the teacher will have encouraged them to be confident in riding a change of rein with a change of lead using a few steps of trot. It is now time for the teacher to consider how the leg on which the horse lands can be influenced even at this early stage in rider education. The simplest approach is for the rider to look in the direction of the next turn. If, for example, the rider is jumping a cross pole on the left rein and wishes to circle left, the rider should look left as the horse begins his descent; this may be enough to ensure that the rider's weight is distributed so that the horse lands on the correct lead. If this fails and the teacher feels that the pupil is sufficiently progressed the rider can open the inside rein to encourage the correct lead on landing. Some horses will always land on one particular leg and with older horses this may be difficult, if not impossible, to correct. In these cases the rider must decide on the best moment to effect the change of lead through trot. The horse must be allowed to get away from the fence, but the transition must not be left so long that there is not sufficient time to re-establish canter before the next fence.

A good exercise for raising rider awareness of landing on the correct lead is to ask the riders to shout out which leg the horse is leading on as soon as they know after landing over the fence. Later on they can do this with their eyes closed, provided that there are no obstacles in the way. This can first be done in the manège by asking the riders to turn down the centre line, close their eyes and ask for canter, call out the lead and turn in the appropriate direction. The exercise is fun, improves the canter aids and the other riders can join in by observing each other. This is an exercise where placing the riders in a line and each rider performing individually has benefits as the teacher can nominate one of the other riders to check that the rider demonstrating is giving correct information. It is also safer to have only one horse out at a time.

Warming-up

This text refers to the course plan diagram on page 81. The course is designed to be used for both warming up and practising jumping a round.

It is a good idea for riders to warm up for a 'course riding' session in the arena

Training show jumping course plan.

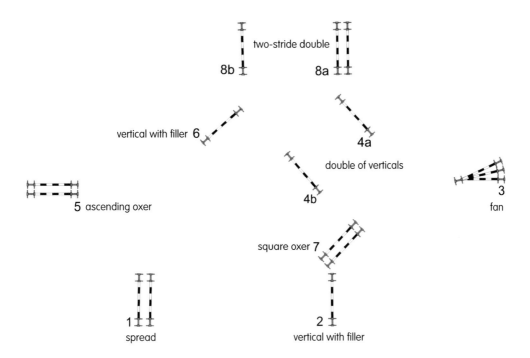

amongst the fences so that they can test the horse's reaction to the fences and other distractions such as vehicles, umbrellas, blowing rubbish, etc. It also gives them a chance to try out the turns that will occur when they are actually jumping. Riders should work in for 15–20 minutes using walk, rising trot, light-seat canter, turns, circles and checking the horse's responsiveness to the aids through transitions. A rider who prefers to start in trot can do so but must then ensure the quality of the canter and the strict maintenance of the balanced seat throughout; this cannot be overemphasised.

The teacher should then introduce a cross pole in trot or canter. In the case of the course in the diagram, fence 1 can be adjusted to a cross pole and jumped off either rein as a warm-up fence. As there are other fences in the arena the riders must have thought about where they are going, both on the approach and the landing. The line or track they are going to follow should be one that encourages the horse to stay in balance and rhythm.

The riders can then progress to fence 2, a vertical with a filler. They should be encouraged to concentrate on the canter rhythm by counting aloud on the way to the fence and resuming counting on landing to help them maintain the same rhythm and tempo. The teacher should try to keep all the riders on the move, allowing them to jump the fence twice and then walk. Obviously they should 'come again' if the jump has not been satisfactory. This should be done from both reins. The riders can now move on to fence 5, an ascending oxer. The emphasis should be on an upbeat canter with plenty of energy but not too fast; approximately 320m per minute (approx.12mph).

After the warm-up the riders should be asked to consider how they anticipate that the course will ride for them. When previously walking the course, they should have paid attention to:

- The distances in the doubles.

- The related distances.

- The track, i.e. the line from one fence to the next.

- The fillers – will they 'spook' the horse?

- Are there any turns which may pose a problem?

- Where will a change of lead be necessary?

- Will the horse hang towards the collecting ring or stables?

For each horse and rider combination the teacher needs to consider:

- The distances.

- Will the horse need to be kept energetic?

- Will the horse need to be kept calm?

The fences should all be well within the riders' capabilities which should enable them to concentrate on these finer points.

Use of the whip

A rider who anticipates that their horse is likely to spook should know how to deal with this. The rider may simply increase the leg pressure as the horse is turned into the fence. Alternatively, if the horse is a slow-reacting, lethargic type the rider may give a slap with the whip. The whip is primarily an aid to back-up the rider's leg; however, there may be times when the whip is used to reprimand a horse, for example if he refuses to jump a fence. In these cases the whip should be used with discretion and must never leave a mark on the horse.

Riders have two main options for using the whip effectively. First, the whip can be used down the horse's shoulder to attract his attention, but this should not be done within the last three strides before a fence or it may actually distract the horse from the task in hand. The rider must be careful that the horse does not veer away from the whip. If the horse has a tendency to turn right then the whip should be in the right hand and vice versa. Second, if the horse refuses for no apparent reason he should be turned slightly away from the fence and, with the reins in one hand, given one or two sharp slaps behind the rider's leg and then re-presented to the fence. It is not advisable to stand the horse in front of the fence and then hit him because:

- The rider cannot allow the horse to go forwards, which is the whole idea of using the whip; and

- It is not permitted under the rules of show jumping as it constitutes showing the horse the fence.

It is not recommended that the novice rider wears spurs. (Riders should learn to be effective without spurs and only use them when they are thoroughly competent and in control of their aids.) The whip should be specifically designed for jumping with a broad, flat end which will reduce the chances of marking the horse. Long dressage whips should only be used by very experienced riders to help with a specific schooling problem.

Having established reasonable proficiency in the preparation work the rider is probably ready now to start riding courses at shows.

Riding out

Hacking

As the competence and confidence of the rider develop, hacking out can be a most enjoyable way of putting new-found skills into practice 'in the field'. In the early stages it is essential that riders are mounted on well-mannered horses who are well within their level of ability. Hacking out for the first time can feel a bit like swimming out of one's depth. Riders have to believe in their ability to cope when there are no safe, confining walls – the equivalent, when swimming, of being able to touch bottom.

It is wise for riders to hack out in pairs or groups, and this usually adds to the enjoyment. However, a rider who is hacking alone should always ensure that someone is aware of where they are going and roughly how long they are likely to be gone. They should take some money with them, and preferably a mobile phone, which can be useful in the event of an emergency. Horse and rider should wear high-visibility clothing. When hacking alone, the rider should take a familiar route on a horse they have ridden out before.

In many parts of Britain, there are some beautiful parts of the countryside accessible to riders – bridle paths, Forestry Commission land, and beaches can all be potential riding areas. Some forestry land may require the rider to hold a current annual pass for access but such information is readily obtainable by riders who live in the locality.

Bridle paths often traverse farm land, common land or moorland. Whatever the case, the rider has responsibility in all instances of off-road riding to respect gates and access points and close them as appropriate. Riders must take great care when crossing fields which have livestock in them. The bridle path will often stay close to the perimeter or headland of the field and this must be adhered to. Occupied fields should be crossed slowly – usually at walk – to avoid disturbing the animals. It is essential not to frighten livestock, particularly in-lamb ewes or milking cows, and cause them to 'run' – serious damage or even loss of life can result, for which the rider would be liable.

Awareness of the countryside can be raised and knowledge enhanced by hacking out; it also helps in developing greater skill and confidence as a rider. Experiencing differing terrain and gradients, coupled with the feeling of the greater power that the horse may give through being unconfined and in wide open spaces, should all increase the rider's ability and enjoyment. It is essential, however, that an experienced rider is always in charge of one or more less competent riders, so that confidence and authority can continue to emanate from the leader. If a number of less experienced riders are taken out for a hack then it is advisable to have more than one competent escort.

Hacking out can range from a simple hour's ride around a local loop, to a longer ride of several hours' duration. In the latter case it is more important to plan the route carefully and perhaps involve a stop at a friendly pub for lunch or a snack. If long rides are planned, the riders and the horses must be fit enough, and perhaps would need to take some precautions against changeable or inclement weather. Riding out for longer than a day can become a challenging and enjoyable holiday option at home or abroad.

Roadwork

Many riders over the last few centuries have ridden on roads to develop their horses' stamina, fitness and to harden/strengthen their legs. Historically, before the modern age of motorised transport, coach horses travelled the countryside in all directions, completing many miles in one work period. These days, many riders still use roadwork for fittening and recreational purposes, although for the latter many new aspects must be seriously considered.

Many of today's roads are heavily overloaded with traffic, and certainly the main arterial routes are totally unsuitable for recreational riding. While country roads remain much quieter, every rider needs to be aware of the potential dangers of riding horses on the road.

Today's cars are fast and powerful, and drivers are often in too much of a hurry to reach their destination. Many drivers, particularly those from urban areas, have no experience of horses and are totally unaware of the hazards involved in meeting one or more horses on the road.

If a rider is going to ride on the road, either for fittening, pleasure or to connect bridleways or other off-road riding routes, then certain precautions need to be taken to try to ensure safety. It is absolutely vital that horses taken on the road are traffic-proof. Most horses, through careful introduction and training, will learn to accept cars and other vehicles in a calm way. The early training must initially involve the young horse seeing vehicles in his home environment – for example, cars in the yard, perhaps the farrier's van or a tractor used for harrowing the fields or arena. From accepting these vehicles, the young horse should then be hacked on quiet roads on the inside or behind a schoolmaster who is very reliable on the road and with traffic. The youngster will then learn to tolerate vehicles passing him as he takes his example from the lead horse.

A few horses find heavy traffic (e.g. tractors and lorries) altogether too frightening and try to turn and run away from such horrors. From experience, most horses reacting in this way do so because of an earlier unfortunate confrontation on the road, giving reason to their fears. In the interests of safety, it is recommended that unreliable horses are not taken onto the road.

The rider also needs to develop experience and confidence on the road. Nervous riders make nervous horses, and the combination is dangerous. A rider with an intrinsic fear of roadwork is better staying in an arena or in off-road situations. Initial road riding should be in the company of an experienced rider on a safe, confident horse.

Riders must learn their responsibilities as road users. One of the best ways to do this is to train for and take the British Horse Society Riding and Road Safety Test. Preparation for and attainment of the certificate of competence will educate the rider in all aspects of roadcraft and safety. A comprehensive booklet entitled *Riding and Roadcraft*, published by the British Horse Society, contains all the relevant information.

As a road user on a horse, just as in a vehicle, courtesy and consideration for other road users leads to harmony and understanding between all participants.

In conclusion:

- Safe off-road riding is the ideal place for recreational riding.

- Roadwork is still a viable option for riding in certain parts of the countryside.

- Roadwork is still regarded by many as an essential part of fittening competition horses.

Riding uphill.   Riding downhill.

Riding up and down hills

Riding up and down hills requires balance and feel so that the rider can assist the horse in negotiating the gradient. As more security of position develops the rider will be better able to cope with differing terrain when riding out or hacking.

It is usually easier to adapt to riding up or down hill by taking up slightly shorter stirrup leathers, rather more towards a jumping length. The closed angle between the lower leg and thigh, and that between the thigh and upper body, will better enable the rider to follow the changing balance of the horse as he tackles the up or down slope.

Generally, the steeper the gradient up hill, the more the rider needs to incline the body forward, taking weight off the horse's back. The rider's weight is then concentrated more into the lower leg, leaving the horse the freedom to use his hind legs and his back to negotiate the hill. When riding down hill the rider needs to become more upright but without taking more weight into the seat and therefore loading the horse's back.

In hill work the rider must learn to develop a good sense of balance to retain a secure position which is both comfortable and affords a feeling of control, and does not impede the horse's ability to deal with the gradient.

When riding up or down hill the slope should always be ridden straight as this will put less strain on the horse's limbs and joints than if the slope is traversed at an angle (i.e. obliquely).

Opening and closing gates

This can be a necessary practical task when riding in the countryside or when going from roads to fields or back. As in much of the information given in this book, there is a requirement for both horse and rider to learn how to perform the task and to gain competence through practice. It is essential that any gate is left secured in the way it was found, particularly if there are stock in the fields.

Gates can be opened mounted or dismounted. Usually the choice is governed by how securely the gate is fastened and how awkward it is to handle from the horse's back.

Opening and closing a gate – mounted

(This example assumes the gate is on the rider's right and opens away from the rider.) The horse should be positioned alongside/parallel to the gate, with his head just past the opening end of the gate. Putting the reins (and whip if carried) into the left hand, the rider leans forward and down to unfasten the gate with the right hand. The right leg is then used behind the girth to move the horse's hindquarters over; the rider pushes the gate open as he moves sideways.

Opening and closing a gate.

If letting other riders through, once the gate is open wide enough, the rider opening the gate asks the horse to stand still to allow the ride to pass. Either keeping hold of the gate, or pushing it away wide, the rider then takes their horse quietly through the gate making sure that if the gate is free it doesn't swing closed and catch the horse on his hindquarters. The gate is then caught or controlled to close it, again with the horse positioned parallel to the gate while the latch is secured.

Opening and closing a gate – dismounted

Sometimes it is impossible to deal with a gate from the horse's back. The gate may need lifting, it may be fixed by a securely tied rope or there may an unwieldy chain at an awkward height. In such cases dismounting is a necessity.

If in a group, the other riders should give the person operating the gate space to manoeuvre – their horse must not be at risk of being kicked or trodden on by others close by. If the area is confined with, say, overhanging branches, the rider dealing with the gate should pass their stirrups over the front of the saddle before dismounting, to prevent them being caught on anything. (This is a wise precaution and a useful habit to adopt under all circumstances.)

Whether the reins are taken over the horse's head or left around his neck will depend on: (a) whether the horse is wearing a running martingale or not; (b) how much room there is to manoeuvre; and (c) how cooperative and biddable the horse is.

If the horse is wearing a martingale, there is not much space and the horse is very leadable, then the reins should be left around his neck. The gate can be dealt with while the horse is held, and then he can be carefully guided back or sideways as necessary using voice and hand pressure. As before, if the gate is being opened, the other riders should be allowed through while the gate-opener's horse is kept still and out of the way of passing horses.

Once they have passed through, the other riders should stay still and close by until the person who dismounted has secured the gate and is safely back in the saddle and has re-taken stirrups and reins.

6. The Theory of the Aids

AIDS ARE THE LANGUAGE OF HORSEMANSHIP and, like all languages, have a basic structure, but it is emphasis and timing which lend them expression and refinement.

It is essential that anyone who wishes to ride well should understand the use, the reasons for, and the effect of the aids, before trying to teach them to a horse. The horse must be taught stage by stage and with complete clarity until the rapport between rider and horse is built up to such a level that it appears that the rider has but to think for the horse to obey willingly. This is the essence of true horsemanship. A trainer who can combine intelligence with mental and physical control and coordination can produce a highly trained, alert and happy horse, working with ease and with complete confidence in his rider.

Aids are the signals or means by which riders convey their wishes to a horse. The term 'aid' thus refers to any action by the rider which results in physical or mental communication between rider and horse.

Aids are sub-divided into natural and artificial as follows:

- Natural aids. The rider's voice, legs, seat and hands.

- Artificial aids. Whips, spurs and any form of strap (other than the reins) which controls or positions the horse, with or without the rider's help. Examples are standing or running martingales, draw or running reins. Only the whip and spur have a place in classical equitation and these are the only artificial aids considered in this chapter.

Natural aids

The voice

The voice by its tone can encourage, correct, soothe or reward. It is also used to give commands, particularly on the lunge and with a young horse when he is first ridden. The horse learns that sharp, quick commands 'walk on', 'trot', 'canter' mean to go forward, and slow and drawn-out 'whoa', 'wa-alk','ter-rot' to reduce the speed or gait. Intonation of the voice upwards for a transition to a faster gait (e.g. from trot to canter) and downwards for a transition to a slower gait (e.g. trot to walk) will add further authority to the aid.

The legs, seat and hands

Although they are discussed separately below, the legs, seat and hands are always used in conjunction with one another as explained in the next chapter.

The legs

The major functions are:

- To produce forward movement.
- To activate the hindquarters.
- To indicate direction and to control the position of the horse.
- To move the horse laterally (sideways).

Identical use of the legs

The effect of using both legs by the girth is to encourage the horse to move forward. When first handled, any horse will react to human contact by withdrawing from it. As flight is his natural defence, when first mounted and feeling the legs of the rider enclosing his rib cage, the reaction is to move forward away from the pressure. This is the basis of all training and is developed and refined by constant repetition, until the slightest pressure with the inside of the rider's legs will result in the horse moving forward.

Individual use of the legs

Once this reaction of moving forward is established, the application of either of the rider's legs by the girth will encourage the horse to move the hind leg forward on that side. Since it will also be instinctive for the horse to try to evade the pressure on the ribs he will also tend to bring the leg forward and slightly under the weight of the body preparatory to turning the hindquarters away from the point of stimulus. This effect is used to move the horse laterally, but if it is not desired, and the horse is required simply to turn a corner, then the rider prevents the hindquarters falling out by placing the other leg slightly further back from the girth. Hence, while both legs cause the horse to go forward, the rider's inside leg by the girth accentuates the forward movement while the outside leg, slightly behind the girth, controls the hindquarters.

Response to the leg aids

The lower legs must always remain in quiet, soft contact with the horse's sides. When a particular signal is required, the legs are used with a vibrant, changing pressure and not a constant squeeze. They should be applied as lightly as possible and only when required, as repeated heavy thumping with the legs, heels or spurs will cause the horse to become dead to the leg.

NB A horse who reacts to leg aids by drawing back is said to be 'behind the leg', and a horse who goes freely forward at the slightest indication from the rider's legs is said to be 'in front of the leg'.

The seat, including the weight

The major influences are on:

- Impulsion.

- Outline.

- Direction.

Use of seat and weight aids

The seat aids can be used beneficially only if the rider can sit correctly, softly and quietly with the weight equally on both seat bones. The rider must allow the horse to remain supple and to swing his back. The novice rider should concentrate on using the seat only insofar as it allows the horse's movement to go 'through': i.e. allows the horse's back muscles to operate freely so that the actions of the hindquarters and forehand are coordinated and not separated by a stiff back. Thus the rider should not sit heavily and stiffly, which would suppress the movement 'through' the horse's back and make the outline hollow. Once a rider can really feel the actions of the horse's hind legs and has developed a seat independent enough to be able to apply an aid without setting up undesired changes or movements elsewhere in the body, then the seat aids can be employed more fully.

These aids can be used in the following ways:

- To lighten the weight on the seat bones and allow the horse's back to come up.

- To allow the horse's back muscles to swing by sitting passively with supple hips.

- To request the desired rhythm.

- In conjunction with the back and lower legs to engage the hindquarters and bring the hind legs more underneath.

On a young horse the weight must be used with great care: if it is not, the horse will hollow and tighten his back. This is why on a young horse most of the early trot work is done rising and much of the first canter work with the rider in a slightly forward seat, off the horse's back. This is particularly important with Thoroughbreds. On the more trained horse, going in a correct round outline, the weight and the use of the back become very important aids.

On straight lines the rider's weight must be absolutely central.

On turns, circles, lateral work and in canter the weight is brought slightly to the inside by turning the body in the direction of the movement and putting more weight into the inside stirrup.

The hands

The major influences are to:

- Contain the impulsion produced by the rider's legs and seat. (Impulsion is the energy produced by the activity of the hindquarters.)

- Control the speed.

- Help the balance.

- Indicate direction.

- Control the bend and aid maintenance of outline.

The hands are only supplementary and complementary to the seat and leg aids. The rider should apply the leg (and seat) aids before the hands, otherwise the hindquarters will tend to fall out behind and the impulsion will be lost rather than contained. As already stated, the use of the seat must be established gradually with a very young horse.

Response to hand aids

Through the reins and the bit the hands are a 'telephone' to the horse's brain and their use has a paramount effect on his mental and physical attitude. To be most effective the hands should:

- Never pull backwards.

- Remain still in relation to the movement of the horse and entirely independent of the action of any other part of the rider's body.

- Maintain a consistent, light, sympathetic but elastic contact with the bit (except when riding on a loose rein). The horse loses his sense of security if the rein contact is inconsistent.

- Keep the same weight in walk, trot and canter, taking care not to make the contact stronger in the faster gaits.

Individual use of the hands

The tension in the reins may not be the same in both hands when working on turns or circles, at the canter, and when correcting the natural crookedness of the horse. It is when working a straight horse on straight lines at the walk and trot that the rider should have an even feel in both hands. For most of the time the reins should be used as follows:

- Outside hand. The hand on the opposite side to the rider's inside leg will receive some of the impulsion sent forward from the horse's inside hind leg. To control this the rider maintains a positive contact with the horse, i.e. one that neither releases nor pulls back the rein but maintains a consistent, sympathetic contact in relation to the movement and therefore goes with it.

- Inside hand. The inside hand accepts and guides the inside bend of the horse, a bend which is created by the rider's seat and leg aids. The contact should be light and flexible to encourage the relaxation of the horse's lower jaw and the acceptance of the bit.

The principle is that the outside hand maintains a positive contact which controls the speed/gait and assists the balance, while the inside hand is more flexible and indicates the bend.

Riding on a long and on a loose rein

A horse can be ridden on a long rein, but the rider should maintain impulsion with the legs and seat while allowing the horse to relax and to stretch forward and down with his head and neck and to lengthen his stride. In walk, for example, the rider, by opening the fingers, lets the reins slide as the horse asks for the extra length but does not completely lose contact. This is known as a free walk on a long rein.

There are times when a horse is ridden on a loose rein without any contact at all. The only connection between the hand and mouth is through the weight of the rein alone. A walk on a loose rein is ridden in the same way as a walk on a long rein, but all contact with the horse's mouth is abandoned and the horse is kept straight by the use of the rider's seat and legs alone. Work on a long and loose rein may be used at all three gaits, provided impulsion and balance are maintained.

On a long rein.

On a loose rein.

Methods of holding the reins

There are many different but acceptable methods of holding the reins. Some of the main ones are mentioned and illustrated on the following pages.

In most methods of holding the reins, the reins run from the horse's mouth, through the fingers, across the palm of the hand and out between the thumb and forefinger, with the thumb on top of the rein. The hand must be lightly closed. In all cases it is the pressure of the thumbs on the reins over the forefingers which prevents the reins from slipping, and not the grip of a clenched hand or fingers.

- **Snaffle bridle.** When held in both hands, the reins pass between the third and fourth fingers, across the palm of the hand and out between the first finger and thumb; alternatively, the reins go round the outside of the little finger and out

Snaffle reins held in one hand.

Snaffle reins held in both hands.

between the first finger and the thumb. When held in one hand, the most commonly used methods are to put the rein being moved between the thumb and first finger and out at the bottom of the hand, or to put it between the second or third finger and out between the first finger and thumb.

- **Double bridle.** When held in both hands, three recommended methods are:

  1. The bridoon rein passes outside the little finger, and the curb, or bit rein, between the third and little finger. Both reins then cross the palm of the hand and go out between the first finger and thumb. This is the most usual way of holding the reins of a double bridle.

  2. As in 1 above, except that the position of the bridoon and bit reins are reversed.

  3. Both bit reins are held in one hand, separated by the second or third finger. The bridoon rein, on that side, passes outside the little finger. All three reins pass out between the first finger and thumb. The other bridoon rein is held between the fingers of the other hand.

     The bit reins are adjusted to the required length on taking them up between the fingers and thereafter are not altered, the horse being ridden on the bridoon reins in each hand.

     A rider who wishes to hold the reins in one hand – e.g. the left hand – has only to transfer the right snaffle rein to the left hand, placing it over the top of the index finger and allowing the slack to hang down from the palm.

The most usual way of holding the reins of a double bridle.

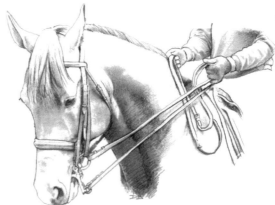

An alternative method of holding the reins of a double bridle. Here the positions of the bridoon and bit reins are reversed.

The artificial aids

The whip

The whip helps to reinforce the leg aids should they prove insufficient. It should be used quickly and lightly behind the leg to emphasise the aid or to ask for more attention.

On occasion it will be necessary to change the hand in which the whip is held. The procedure with a long schooling whip is to put the reins into the hand holding the whip, and the free hand then takes hold of the whip below the holding hand, the back of the hand towards the rider's body. The whip is brought quietly across to the other side with the tapered end of the whip passing in front of the rider's face; the rein is then retaken by the whip hand.

An alternative method, and one that is more appropriate for a short 'jumping type' whip, is to put the reins into the hand holding the whip; then the free hand takes hold

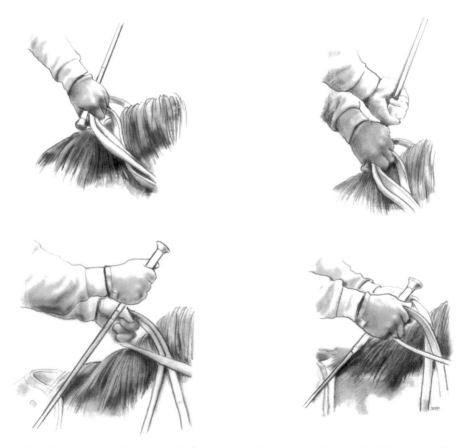

Changing a schooling/dressage whip from one hand to the other (see text for fuller explanation).

Changing a short whip from one hand to the other (see text for fuller explanation).

of the whip above the holding hand, and draws it through the hand. The whip is then brought quietly across to the other side, tapered end downwards. The reins are then picked up again.

The **schooling whip** is used for schooling on the flat. It should be between 0.90m (3ft) and 1.2m (4ft) in length so that it is long enough to apply without taking the hand off the rein. The wrist is flicked to result in a tickle or a tap whenever required, behind the rider's leg.

The **shorter whip**, used for jumping, must not exceed 75cm (just under 30in). The whip hand should be taken off the rein, and both reins should be held in one hand and the whip applied behind the leg. The rider should practise this action and the ability to change whip hands with each type of whip.

Spurs

Spurs are regarded as an artificial aid in the same category as the whip. They may be introduced when the horse has accepted the concept of reacting to the leg aid and should permit a more refined reaction to the leg. It is important that the rider's position is secure and independent, and that the rider can fully control the application of the legs. Spurs are rarely used in the early training of a horse and are not suitable for use by inexpert horsemen.

The spur position on the back of the rider's boot, in the region of the ankle joint, should enable a light aid to be given on the horse's flank, as required. When used, the spur should only brush the skin. At no stage should the spur be constantly jabbing at the horse's side, with the rider's leg gripping on. In this case the spur could mark or damage the horse's side, which would be unacceptable and abusive.

Spurs are a refinement of the aids and should not be used as a sole means of producing impulsion. The rider must be able to apply leg aids without the spurs touching the horse.

Whilst spurs are mandatory in dressage competitions of Medium level and above, they are optional at lower levels. Much depends on the horse's natural responsiveness to the aids. Lazy horses can benefit from being ridden in spurs. Sometimes, though, it is wise to vary the times when spurs are worn (e.g. not always when schooling) so that the horse stays responsive to their use.

Spurs vary in size and severity – some are very small, smooth and rounded, whilst others are longer, more angular or with rowels. Restrictions on certain types of spur are made in some competitions, so check the rules before competing.

Practical use of the aids

The aids and movements can be used in every form of riding. The horse will often be required to carry out some of the schooling movements, not merely as an exercise, or part of a dressage test, but for strictly practical reasons. For example, when out hacking, besides the obvious necessity of the aids for changing direction or altering speed or gait, the turn on the forehand, the half-pirouette and the rein-back may be used when opening and closing gates, and a rider can help to prevent the horse from shying by using the shoulder-in.

Summary

- The aim is for the aids to encourage the horse to go forward, straight and with rhythm.
- Ride from the inside leg into the outside rein.
- Use inside leg for impulsion, close to the girth.
- Use outside leg for controlling the quarters, a little back.
- Use inside rein for direction and bend.
- Use outside rein for balance, controlling speed and regulating bend.
- Keep weight to inside in turns, circles and lateral work.

- Turn body in direction of movement.

- Always keep body upright.

Good aids are those which:

- Ensure that the forward impetus of the horse is given willingly and completely into the rider's control.

- Dictate the speed, gait and/or the direction of the movement.

- Are unobtrusive.

Aids are misused if they:

- Position or restrain the horse's body or speed by force.

- Produce more impulsion than the rider can control.

- Fail to produce the impulsion needed to help the horse to accept the bit.

- Fail to allow the rider's weight to move in harmony with that of the horse.

- Fail to allow the hands to follow the horse's movement.

- Are neither definite nor clear enough for the horse to comprehend their meaning.

- Are used continually, even involuntarily and without reason or anticipation.

- Are used roughly, obviously, or to punish without justification.

7. The Use of the Aids

THIS CHAPTER DESCRIBES HOW RIDERS USE THE AIDS to convey their wishes to the horse. The aids are comparatively few but the way in which they are applied – for example, the degree of pressure of each leg and of contact in each rein – can vary greatly, and their use calls for skill and tact on the part of the rider.

For the aids to be most effective the rider must be in balance, and this is best achieved by establishing the correct position.

For fuller definitions of the movements, refer to the British Dressage's *Rules for Dressage*, and the Fédération Equestre Internationale's (FEI's) *Rules for Dressage Events*.

The terms **'inside'** and **'outside'** are used frequently and refer to the slight curve throughout the length of the horse's body, 'inside' always being the concave side of the horse when correctly bent, and vice versa; they do not refer to the sides of the school or manège.

Forward movement

In all forward movement it is essential for the rider to look ahead at the point towards which the horse is being asked to move.

The first aid used by the rider is to activate the horse's hind legs into forward movement. To achieve this into the walk or trot (often referred to as 'moving off' or 'going forward into'); or into the canter (usually called 'striking off'), or for other upward transitions, the aids are as follows.

Moving off and upward transitions

The rider:

- Checks position.

- Maintains a light contact through the reins with the horse's mouth.

- Applies extra pressure with both legs by the girth – not a steady squeeze but a series of quick, vibrant touches with the inside of the calf muscles.

- Advanced riders, who are able to feel the natural inclination of their horse to favour a left or right bend, may compensate for this when moving off into a faster gait by adopting the opposite position: e.g. position right on a horse with a preference for a left bend. (See 'Position right and left', page 104). This helps to maintain suppleness and keeps the horse straight.

Striking off into canter

The rider:

- Checks position.

- Asks the horse for position right or left according to which leading leg is required. (See pages 109–110).

- Applies the outside leg back behind the girth to encourage the horse's hind leg on that side to move forward and so to start the sequence of the canter gait (pages 109–110).

- Applies the inside leg by the girth to encourage forward movement.

- Moves the inside seat bone forward, and when the canter is established the weight comes slightly to that inner side.

- Moves the weight a little to the inside.

- Takes care to keep the horse straight and not allow the quarters to move to the inside.

Controlling the forward movement

The reins are used to control the forward movement, but except in the case of a very young horse their action must be in conjunction with the legs and seat aids in order to keep the hindquarters engaged. These rein aids are applied through sympathetic movement of the fingers and the hands.

It is easy for riders to become over-focused on the contact or weight of the rein. They should aim to remember that the feel in the rein relates directly to the activity from the hind legs!

The half-halt (see also page 150)

This is a hardly visible moderated version of the halt (see page 103) – 'the momentary collection of a horse in motion' (Von Blixen-Finecke).

The rider:

- Applies momentarily the driving aids of the seat and the legs.

- Uses the hands to restrain momentarily the horse's consequent desire to go forward so that the horse becomes more collected, rather than going faster.

- Releases momentarily the pressure on the reins before restoring the original contact.

- The horse is enclosed briefly between the weight, leg and rein aids before the hands yield again.

- The half-halt may be repeated as frequently as required to concentrate the energy into the hind legs and increase the horse's desire to go forward more confidently into the bridle.

Upward transitions within a gait

For transitions from collected to working, medium or extended gaits:

The rider:

- Checks position.

- Makes a half-halt to get the horse's hind legs more engaged.

- Applies the legs by the girth to lengthen the stride.

- With the reins, while containing the impulsion, allows the horse to lengthen his outline.

- Maintains a supple seat, through movement of the loins and hip joints, thus allowing the horse to swing through his back.

NB At the trot, during training, it is often advisable to rise.

Downward transitions

The rider:

- Checks position.

- Makes one or more half-halts with the outside rein or with both reins; the former is more acceptable as long as the contact on the inside rein is consistently maintained and the bit is not moved through the horse's mouth.

- Uses the legs and seat to engage the hind legs and lower the quarters so that the horse's forehand is lightened.

- Uses the reins as little as necessary with a restraining but not restrictive movement. The slowing-down aid is usually given with the outside rein.

- As soon as the new gait is established, rides forward by the use of the seat and legs ensuring that the rhythm of that new gait is maintained.

- Takes care that position and balance are maintained; there must be no unbalancing forward of the movement.

The halt *(see also page 151)*

The aids are the same as for all downward transitions, but in this case the restraining but allowing hands finally stop the movement. Even in the halt impulsion should not be allowed to escape, so the horse maintains a light contact with the bit and the rider's legs remain on the horse's side.

It is important, not just in connection with halt, but in respect of transitions generally, that the concept of 'restraining but allowing hands' is understood. While restraining the rider closes the fingers firmly around the reins (without pulling) thereby encouraging the horse to yield to the contact. Once the horse has yielded it is important for the rider to release without losing the contact on the reins and softly allow the horse to take the contact forward. It is important for the rider at all times to ride the horse forward from the leg aids. The restraining aids should be used in transitions and when the horse has lost his balance. When the transition has been successfully completed or the balance restored, the rider's hands remain still and passive.

Turns and circles *(see also illustration on page 39/bottom right)*

In turns and circles the horse remains bent around the rider's leg. His hind legs should follow exactly in the track of the forelegs. This is achieved by riding from the inside leg into the outside rein.

So to turn or circle:

The rider:

- Checks position.

- Applies the fingers on the inside rein intermittently, to establish a more flexible contact and a slight bend, and thus indicate direction.

- Turns the body to the inside and transfers slightly more weight into the inside stirrup.

- Uses the outside rein to allow the bend of the horse's head and neck with a constant contact (unless bringing it into use to control the impulsion and the extent of the bend).

- Uses both legs and a supple seat to maintain impulsion, but the inside leg by the girth dominates and must be sufficiently effective to induce the horse to bring his hind leg, on that side, forward and slightly under the centre of his body; only then will the horse be able to follow the true line of the circle.

- Rests the outside leg slightly back. The leg remains in this position ready for use if the horse's hindquarters start to swing to the outside of the circle.

- Is very careful not to increase the weight of the inside rein.

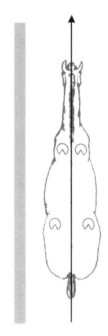

Straight.

Position right and left

A rider is said to be in position right when the right leg is close to the girth, and the left leg a little behind the girth, therefore indicating a slight bend with the right rein and controlling the impulsion, speed and bend with the left rein. The rider is then said to be riding from the inside leg into the outside rein. In position left the aids are reversed.

The rider spends much time in position right or left with the need to combat the horse's natural crookedness; also because of the frequency of turns, the action of the horse at the canter, and as a preparation for many movements.

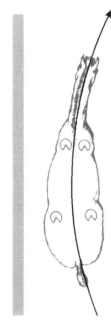

Correct bend through the horse's body. Hind leg tracks corresponding foreleg.

PART 2

TRAINING THE HORSE

8. The Gaits

TO TRAIN A HORSE CORRECTLY it is essential to maintain the purity of the gaits rather than to create or fail to correct the numerous defects which develop in the horse's movements. Therefore, the trainer must understand the way the horse should move at the walk, trot canter and gallop and for each of these gaits the sequence of the leg movements is different, as is the rhythm of the hoof beats.

The walk

Rhythm

Four hoof beats should be heard at equal intervals. The horse moves one leg after another so that the four hoof beats can be heard with the same period between each. Two or three feet are always on the ground at the same time, the horse stepping from one foot to another with no moment of suspension.

Sequence in which the legs leave the ground

Left hind leg: left foreleg; right hind leg; right foreleg.

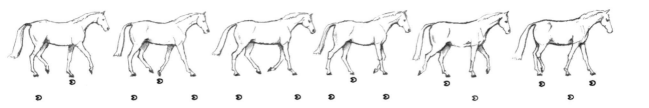

The sequence of footfalls at the walk.

The aims

- Rhythm of hoof beats is regular with the four beats distinctly marked. (Any losses of regular four-time hoof beats is incorrect. This includes a two-time walk, known as a pace or amble).

- The strides are even and not hurried.

- The strides are free, purposeful and unconstrained.

- The head nods in the walk. The rider should not restrict this movement.

- The feet are lifted, not dragged along the ground.

NB Faults in the walk are easily developed, as there is little impulsion to help the rider maintain the rhythm of the gait. It is, therefore, not advisable to walk 'on the bit' during the early stages of training.

The trot

Rhythm

Two hoof beats should be heard, with the legs moving in alternate diagonal pairs, but separated by a moment of suspension. This moment of suspension is difficult for the inexperienced rider to sit to, and the problem can be avoided by rising out of the saddle as one of the diagonal pairs leaves the ground and returning to the saddle as this same pair comes back to the ground (rising trot).

Sequence in which legs leave the ground

1. Right foreleg and left hind leg.

2. Left foreleg and right hind leg before the right foreleg and left hind leg touch the ground.

The sequence of footfalls at the trot.

The aims

- The rhythm of the hoof beats is regular (two-time).

- The strides are even in length and not hurried.

- The strides are light and elastic.

- The hindquarters are engaged.

- The joints flex and the limbs are not dragged.

- The hind feet do not hit the forefeet (forging).

- The head remains steady.

The forelegs should not show more extravagant movement than the hind legs.

The canter

Rhythm

Three hoof beats should be heard and, as with the trot, there is a moment of suspension when all four feet are off the ground.

Sequence in which legs leave the ground

When the right foreleg leads:

1. Left hind leg.

2. Right hind and left foreleg together.

3. Right foreleg followed by a moment of suspension.

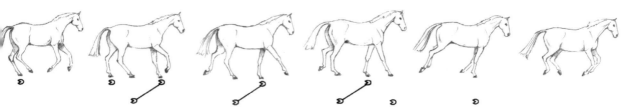

The sequence of footfalls at right canter.

The sequence of footfalls at left canter.

When the left foreleg leads:

1. Right hind leg.

2. Left hind leg and right foreleg together.

3. Left foreleg followed by a moment of suspension.

When the canter is **disunited** (a fault) the forehand is on one lead and the hindquarters are on the other.

The aims

- Rhythm of hoof beats is regular (three-time). Four hoof beats should not be heard, but they often are when a horse is slowed down without sufficient impulsion.

- Strides are even and not hurried.

- Steps are light and cadenced.

- Hindquarters are engaged, with active hocks.

- Balance is maintained.

- Horse is straight, with his shoulders directly in front and not to one side of his hindquarters.

- The canter is true (not disunited).

- Head moves in coordination with the horizontal action of the body. The horizontal movement occurs because when only the leading foreleg is on the ground the hindquarters must rise and the head tip towards the ground, whereas at the end of the moment of suspension the hindquarters drop and the head rises. The result is a bounding action by the horse in the canter.

The gallop

Rhythm

This is the horse's fastest and most extended gait: the diagonal sequence of the canter is broken. It thus becomes a gait in which four hoof beats should be heard, followed by a moment of suspension.

Sequence in which legs leave the ground

When the left foreleg leads:

    1. Right hind leg.

    2. Left hind leg.

    3. Right foreleg.

    4. Left foreleg followed by a moment of suspension.

When the right foreleg leads:

    1. Left hind leg.

    2. Right hind leg,

    3. Left foreleg.

    4. Right foreleg followed be a moment of suspension.

The aims

- Rhythm of hoof beats is regular (four-time).

- Strides are even and not hurried.

- Balance is maintained.

- Horse is straight with his shoulders directly in front and not to one side of his hindquarters.

Variations within a gait

A horse can be asked to extend and/or collect (that is, change the length of his strides and outline) at each gait. The extent of the variations within a gait depends upon the stage of the horse's training, and on his own natural ability.

In the initial training, the horse has not the impulsion or suppleness to collect or extend truly: therefore at the trot and canter the working gaits only should be asked for, and in the walk just the medium and free walk. As the training proceeds progressively, more collection can be demanded and at the same time extension, to achieve first of all the medium trot and canter and eventually, the extended walk, trot and canter.

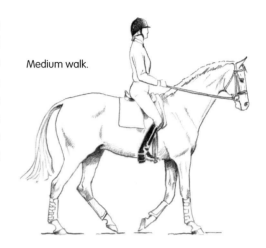

Medium walk.

Aims within these variations

- The collection should result in shorter, rounder strides, not slower ones, and for the extension more ground-covering, longer strides, not quicker ones. When trying to extend the strides hurrying is one of the most common faults and leads to stiffening, which can spoil the gaits. It is nearly always caused by the rider asking the horse to extend before he has enough impulsion to be able to do so.

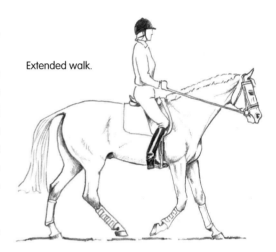

Extended walk.

- The strides should be even: i.e. when the required length of stride has been achieved each stride should be maintained at this length, so that every stride is even.

- The rhythm of the hoof beats of a particular gait should remain true (the walk four-time, the trot two-time and the canter three-time): i.e. the gait should be regular.

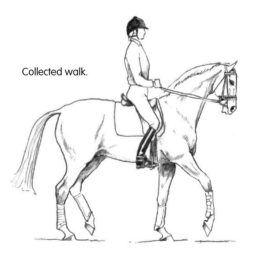

Collected walk.

- In all variations within a gait the horse should retain his willingness to go freely forward.

Working gaits

These are the gaits which lie between the collected and medium. They are used particularly for horses not yet trained and ready for collected gaits. Working walk is not recognised, but the working trot and canter are the gaits from which respectively other trots and canters are developed.

Aims at all working gaits

- To maintain the balance.

- To keep the horse 'on the bit'.

- For the hocks to be active, but this does not mean collection, only the production of impulsion from active hindquarters.

- To produce strides which are free and elastic.

Medium gaits

These are gaits of moderate extension between working and extended.

Aims at all medium gaits

- Longer strides than for working, but rounder and shorter than for extended.

- Unconstrained strides with rhythm and balance.

- To produce lively impulsion from the hindquarters.

- To keep the horse 'on the bit' (see page 140) with the head and neck slightly lower than in the working and collected gaits. To extend the head more in front of the vertical than in the collected and working gaits.

Medium trot.

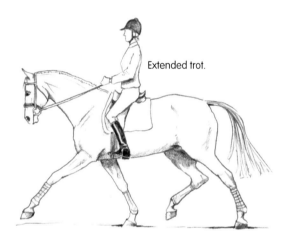

Extended trot.

Collected trot.

Particular features

At the medium walk the hind feet should touch the ground in front of the footprints of the forefeet (overtracking). This is the walk at which the rider first works the young horse.

Extended gaits

In these the horse lengthens his strides to his utmost.

Aims at all extended gaits

- The strides to be as long as possible while maintaining rhythm and balance.

- To produce lively impulsion from the hindquarters. (Although, if extended gaits are used with the intention of improving impulsion, care should be taken that balance is not lost.)

- The horse to remain calm, and light in the forehand.

- To keep the horse on the bit with the head and neck lowered and lengthened so that the strides become longer, rather than higher.

- Not to make hurried strides.

Particular features

At the extended walk, overtracking should be more pronounced than in the medium and the rider should allow the horse to stretch out his head and neck but without losing contact with the mouth. At the extended trot there should be no flicking of the forelegs.

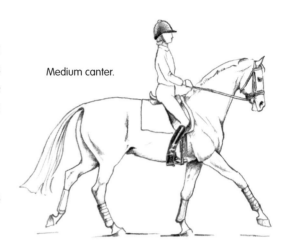

Medium canter.

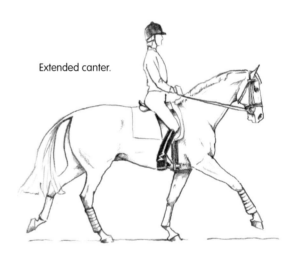

Extended canter.

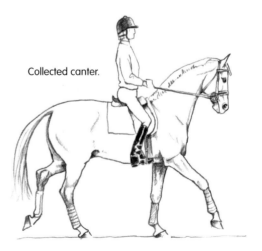

Collected canter.

Collected gaits

In these the strides become shorter and higher and the horse is at his most manoeuvrable.

Aims at all collected gaits

- To produce lively impulsion from the hindquarters, which are strongly engaged with the joints well bent. This should result in a lightening of the forehand and the shoulders becoming more free and mobile.

- To keep the horse on the bit with his neck raised and arched so that there is an harmonious curve from the withers to the highest point – the poll. The head should be slightly in front of the vertical but may become more or less perpendicular when the combined seat, leg and rein aids are applied.

- The hind legs to be engaged.

- The quarters should be lowered.

Particular features

At the collected walk and trot the hind feet should touch the ground behind or in the footprints of the forefeet.

Free gaits

At these the horse is allowed complete freedom to lower and stretch his head and neck. He relaxes, but should remain active. The free walk is the most commonly used, especially for young horses, and as a reward for good work.

9. The Initial Training of the Ridden Horse

IN THE HORSE'S NATURAL STATE his instinctive defence is flight, and he fights only if provoked or cornered. The aim of early training is to overcome his fear, to earn his trust and obedience, and to turn the instinct of flight into a willingness to go forward at all times.

Efforts to do this should start from the time a foal is born, and if they are successful in the early stages they will greatly simplify the horse's subsequent training.

Early handling

A foal should be handled from birth so that he learns to trust and respect humans and not to fear them. In the years before he is ridden he should be trained progressively to:

- Lead quietly.
- Be halter broken and tied up.
- Be groomed and have his feet picked out and trimmed.
- Accept the various items of tack used for backing and riding.
- Become familiar with and learn not to fear a variety of strange sights and sounds.
- Obey the basic commands: e.g. 'walk on','whoa'.

The stages of initial training

When the horse is 3 or 4 years old he should have developed sufficiently – physically and mentally – to undergo the concentrated and progressive training of being backed, ridden and learning the aids.

The stages of training are:

1. Leading in hand.

2. Lungeing.

3. Backing: i.e. teaching the horse to accept a rider on his back.

4. Being ridden on the lead and lunge.

5. Control by the rider.

Feeding during these stages must be carefully monitored. A young horse fed too much carbohydrate in the diet tends to be too spirited to understand and obey. It is vital to keep him sensible, which usually means limiting his feed (unless he is lazy and/or weak), and turning him out to grass whenever possible.

The length of training varies from horse to horse, depending largely on the horse's temperament, the extent and success of his initial handling, and the ability of the trainer.

As a rough guide, and assuming that the early handling of the foal and youngster has been satisfactory, a professional trainer usually takes 4 to 6 weeks to lead, lunge, back and quietly ride a young horse. This applies to training at a school where cost, and therefore time, is usually an important factor. It is essential for training not to be hurried. The horse should never be asked to carry out more than his condition or temperament warrant. Anyone wishing to train their own horse would be well advised to spend much longer on this early work. Extensive work on the lunge pays dividends later on, and up to 12 weeks can be spent on this stage.

Tack *(see also page 128)*

The following tack is needed:

- A lungeing cavesson.

- A snaffle bridle.

- A cotton or nylon webbing lunge rein.

- A roller and breast plate, or a saddle, preferably with numnah and breast plate.

- Side-reins.

- Boots, which should be worn on all four legs in all work.

- A neck strap, if a breast plate is not fitted.

The trainer needs a long lunge whip and should always wear gloves and a hard hat.

Fitting the tack

The items should be introduced one at a time, the horse being allowed to accept each new item quietly and calmly before another is tried.

To fit a lunge cavesson

This should be buckled firmly enough to avoid it being pulled around. The lead/lunge rein is normally fitted to the central ring of the cavesson.

To fit a bridle

The snaffle bit must fit the horse's mouth so that it is neither so narrow that it pinches, nor so wide that the joint falls far down in the horse's mouth. The mouthpiece should be quite thick and single-jointed. Some horses object to having a bridle fitted, however carefully this is done, and in such cases the bridle may be put on like a headcollar with the bit fastened to the off-side cheek piece only and allowed to hang down. The bit can then be put in the horse's mouth very gently before securing the near-side cheek piece firmly enough so that the corners of the horse's mouth just wrinkle. If the bit is too low the horse can easily get his tongue over it, if too high it will be uncomfortable.

To fit a cavesson with a bridle – see page 128.

To fit a roller

Great care is necessary when first fitting a roller and later the saddle, as many horses are very disturbed by the restrictive feeling of the girth. One person is needed to hold the horse's head and also to help with adjustments on the horse's off-side if a third person is not available. The trainer stands on the near-side and places the roller, with the buckle end bent back over itself, very gently on the horse's back. The breast plate is attached to prevent the roller from slipping back, before the buckle end of the girth is slid gently down the horse's off-side, quietly brought under the horse, and drawn up to the retaining straps on the roller. It is attached very loosely at first, but if the horse is not upset it is gradually tightened by one or two holes at a time. It is advisable to move the horse forward a few steps between each tightening operation.

To fit a saddle

The same procedure is followed as for fitting the roller, including the attachment of the breast plate. Initially it is important for the girth to be only just tight enough to prevent the saddle from slipping; if too tight the horse will often buck against the pressure.

Leading in hand

The foal

In most cases a horse is taught to lead in and out of his field or stable alongside his dam. To start with, the foal should be walked around his stable with a stable rubber around his neck, and a hand around his hindquarters. It is important to push rather than pull, helping to instil the willingness to go forward at an early age. Once he understands this, he may be led from a foal slip, but one hand should remain on or around the hindquarters, and it is this hand which deals with any arguments. The foal will soon learn that it is useless to resist and may then be led outside his stable, following his mother.

The young horse

If a young horse has missed this early training he can be taught to lead in a stable, preferably a large one, and it is best not to lead him outside until he is quiet and obedient on both reins.

A young horse should be led by a rein of about 3m (9ft 9in) fastened to the central ring of a lunge cavesson. When the horse is used to a bridle, one may be fitted under the cavesson, but the lead rein should never be attached to the snaffle bit as this may spoil his mouth.

Assistance

In the early stages, unless the horse has been taught to move freely forward as a foal, it is advantageous for the trainer to have an assistant walking behind the horse, who can send the horse forward if he tries to stop or run back.

Technique

The trainer should walk alongside, but not in front, of the horse's shoulder on the near-side, holding a whip, which should be long enough to reach the horse's hindquarters, in the left hand. If the horse draws back, or tries to stop, the trainer can use voice and whip to encourage him forwards (see illustration overleaf). Often the threat of the whip is sufficient to make the horse obey, but if necessary it can be applied gently and, if this is not effective, more strongly. Forward movement is of prime importance in the early and indeed all stages of training. If, however, the young horse tries to hurry or run on too

Use of the whip when the horse is reluctant to be led forward.

much, repeated, rapid jerks on the front of the cavesson, together with the voice, can be used to slow him down or stop.

When the horse accepts being led on the near-side he should be taught to go equally well from the off-side.

Before starting to lunge, the horse should obey the commands to 'walk on' and 'whoa'.

Lungeing and long reining

Lungeing has an essential part to play in the training of the young horse, as long as it is carried out correctly. The next chapter describes in detail the technique of lungeing.

Long reining

In the past, long reining was widely practised as an alternative or supplement to lungeing, before backing was carried out. Although it enables a higher standard of training to be achieved, it requires special skills, and needs an experienced trainer if the young horse is not to be spoilt. The novice trainer should not experiment with long reining on a young horse, but should first learn the technique under the guidance of an expert, using an older horse as a guinea pig.

The stages

1. The horse is tacked up as for lungeing, with bridle, roller, cavesson to which the lunge rein is attached on the central ring, and boots. The trainer carries a lunge whip and first settles the horse, lungeing him in the normal manner.

2. With the trainer holding the lunge rein and standing by the horse's inside shoulder, an assistant attaches a second lunge rein to the side ring on the outside of the cavesson, runs it back through the D on the roller and around the outside of the horse's hindquarters. This must be carried out with great care so that the horse will not be frightened by the feel of the rein. With a nervous horse, some people begin with the rein coming from the D over the horse's back, and progress from there to round the quarters.

3. The trainer is given the second (outside) rein but does not place any tension on this rein until the horse is calm and relaxed. The horse is asked to go forward in a circle around the trainer as on the lunge, with the inside rein acting as a normal lunge rein.

4. The inside rein is attached to the inside ring of the cavesson and run back through the D on the roller as with the outside rein. In work, gradually more pressure is put on the outside rein to develop it as a controlling aid.

5. The horse is asked to change direction, at the walk, the previous outside rein becoming the inside one.

6. The reins are attached to the bit instead of the cavesson.

7. The horse is asked to go forward in straight lines and to turn corners with the trainer behind him.

Whether on a circle or a straight line, the horse can be asked to halt, move off and change his gait.

The time schedule for these stages depends on the temperament of the horse and on how advanced his training is. The essential factor is that the trainer only attempts the next stage if the horse is calm in the easier work.

Long reining is of value with a young horse to teach him the driving and 'steering' aids. It usually helps to establish a confident mouth, which makes control much easier once the horse is backed and ridden. Long reining is also very advantageous in advanced dressage work, as it is a useful aid to achieving collection and lateral work.

Backing

Timing

The trainer must decide when a horse is ready to be backed, according to each individual case. It is generally not attempted until the horse is obedient, relaxed and working well on the lunge.

If the preparatory work has been carried out correctly, the horse should accept the rider quietly and with confidence. Conversely, a horse who reacts violently to being backed has almost certainly been inadequately prepared or has had a previous bad experience.

Equipment

Backing is best carried out in an enclosed place, such as an indoor riding school or a small paddock – a stable is too confined and potentially unsafe. The horse should be fitted with a snaffle bridle under the cavesson, a breast plate, and a saddle, which most trainers prefer without stirrup leathers and irons.

Assistance

If possible, three people should be available: the trainer, who usually holds the horse; an assistant, who helps the rider to mount and dismount and to maintain position on the saddle; and the rider. With an experienced trainer, however, backing can – and often has to be – achieved by two people. The trainer then both helps the rider to mount and holds the horse.

A useful aid is to place a straw bale by the horse for the rider to use as a mounting block and to help accustom the horse to seeing a human above him.

The stages

1. Before starting, the horse should be lunged to settle him. When the horse is relaxed and calm, the trainer stands at the horse's head, on the near-side, holding him by the lunge rein which is attached to the cavesson. The rider, also on the

Legging-up the rider to lean across the saddle.

near-side, takes hold of the saddle, pats it, moves it gently about on the horse's back, jumps up and down a few times and then repeats this with one hand on the pommel and the other on the cantle. The whole procedure should then be repeated on the off-side.

2. If the horse remains calm, the trainer (or assistant, if available) can give the rider a leg-up so that the rider can lean across the saddle (see above). This exercise can be repeated on the off-side. If the horse becomes upset, the trainer should comfort him and the rider can slide quietly to the ground. Whenever possible, the rider, whilst lying across the saddle, pats the horse on the opposite side. To reach this stage on the first day of backing is sufficient progress.

3. When the young horse accepts the rider leaning across the saddle from either side, he can be led forward a few steps – but this position is tiring for the rider and cannot be held for long.

4. The rider can then start to move around a little on the saddle, both at the halt and as the horse is led forward, and can also slowly raise both head and shoulders.

5. As the horse becomes confident, the rider can put a leg over the saddle, taking care not to touch the horse's hindquarters, to sit astride. The top part of the rider's body is still kept low, near to the horse's neck. This is done at the halt, and when

the horse remains calm he can be walked forward a few steps. The rider can then slowly adopt a more upright position so that the horse becomes accustomed to this.

At all times the rider and the trainer must be quick to reward the horse when he does well, by patting him on the neck and praising him. Titbits should be avoided except as a reward at the end of the lesson.

Riding on the lead and lunge

When first ridden the horse is led forward quietly, with the rider sitting upright but relaxed. Control is in the hands of the person leading, who can play out the rein and move away until the horse is on the lunge circle. When the horse walks the circle calmly he can be asked to trot: at first when being led and then on the lunge. The rider starts in sitting trot with very little weight on the seat bones, but uses the rising trot as soon as the action of coming out of the saddle does not alarm the horse.

Equipment

Stirrups are used at the discretion of the rider; some prefer to use them from the start – but with caution, as they can get in the way and upset the horse by banging on his sides. The neck strap or breast plate is always worn and can be used by the rider to maintain a secure position without interfering with the horse's mouth. The reins should be attached to the bit from the beginning, but only used in dire emergencies. Side-reins should never be fitted.

Introducing the aids

If the horse remains calm when being led around the school or paddock with the rider on his back, the aids can be introduced. The trainer, holding the lunge rein loosely, should encourage the horse to walk and halt, first in obedience to the trainer's voice and then to the rider's. The rider can then begin to introduce the rein and leg aids in conjunction with the voice. A schooling whip may be carried by the rider to reinforce when necessary (but with great care) the leg aids. However, depending on the temperament, manner and confidence of the horse, it may be wise to wait until the horse is working independently off the lunge before carrying and introducing a schooling whip.

Control by the rider

When the horse walks, trots, and halts calmly to the rider's aids, the lunge rein can be removed. To ensure a smooth changeover after detaching the rein, the trainer may continue to walk beside the horse, although leaving control to the rider, before moving away gradually.

The rider should concentrate on getting the horse to move forward calmly in answer to the aids, including the voice. When the rider wishes to make a turn it will be necessary to rely more on the use of the reins as the voice will not mean anything in this context. Whilst riding the horse forward, the directional aid for an early turn will entail moving a hand out boldly to the required side, but without any backward tension.

Quiet, clear commands and firm but kind handling should produce results, with the horse obeying the simple aids at walk and trot.

Cantering

There should be no hurry to teach the horse to canter with a rider. If started too early it can excite the young horse and may result in him losing his balance, even to the extent that the sequence of the gait and the length of stride are impaired.

To begin with, cantering should only be asked for on a straight line. On corners the horse can be allowed to fall back into the trot until repetition improves his balance and understanding of what is wanted. The rider merely takes up the correct position and gives encouragement until later when the more serious cantering lessons can start.

It is often easier for a young horse to canter if the rider adopts the basic position for jumping (see upper illustration page 72).

Standing still when mounted

For safety and discipline it is essential for the horse to remain still when mounted, both when the rider is legged-up and when using the stirrup to mount.

An assistant should hold the horse's head to ensure that he does not move when the rider is legged-up and first learns to accept the rider mounting with a foot in the stirrup. These first lessons are best carried out at the end of a riding session so that the horse is relaxed and even a little tired.

As soon as the horse is not disturbed by this manner of mounting, the rider can mount using the stirrups at the beginning of a session, at first with an assistant holding the horse's head, but after a few days without him. Then the rider must keep the horse immobile through use of the voice and, if necessary, the reins.

Acceptance of strange/unusual objects

An essential part of a young horse's training is to get him to accept strange sights and sounds without fear. Even when he is a foal, coloured poles can be placed on the ground at the entrance to his paddock and he can be encouraged to follow his dam over them. It is beneficial, too, to turn him out in a field from which traffic can be seen and heard.

Traffic

Motor vehicles are a serious hazard today and great care must be taken to train the young horse to accept them calmly. It is important to take every possible precaution to prevent him from being frightened by lorries or cars.

When riding outside for the first few times it is advisable to go with one or two trained, quiet horses who can set an example and give confidence. At first the trained horse should be kept between the young horse and the traffic, and if he remains calm, the older horse can go in front of him, and eventually behind.

Shying

If a horse shies at an object, he should not be beaten or forced too close to it, but allowed to pass by at what he considers a safe distance and with his head bent away from it. If each time he passes the object causing concern, the rider can quietly ask him to go a little nearer, the horse should eventually overcome his fear to pass it without shying. In this way any argument can be avoided, and it is more likely that the cure will be permanent.

Summary

When a young horse is able to walk, trot, and canter calmly under the control of his rider, and has had regular ridden exercise for two to three months, he should be sufficiently confident and physically fit to undertake the next stage of training.

10. Lungeing the Horse

LUNGEING CAN BE USED THROUGHOUT THE TRAINING OF THE HORSE. As long as it is done well it improves the horse's physical coordination – developing his rhythm, balance, suppleness, willingness to go forward and fitness; but probably even more important than this, it trains the horse's mind and can be a major influence on his mental outlook. Through lungeing, the horse can be taught to respect, trust and obey his trainer.

The major uses of lungeing are:

- The initial training of the young horse.

- Retraining spoilt horses.

- Exercising horses who are not being ridden.

- Settling and relaxing fresh or spirited horses before they are ridden.

- Advanced dressage work.

- To train the rider (see Chapters 3 and 4).

Lungeing is therefore an essential aspect of work with horses, but if the horse is to derive full benefit, it demands a trainer with considerable experience, skill and ability to anticipate the horse's movements.

Equipment

The lungeing area *(see also page 58)*

An area of flat ground large enough for a circle of at least 20m. It is an advantage if it is enclosed (sheep hurdles, poles, etc., can be used if an arena is not available), and if it is reasonably quiet so that the horse's attention can be maintained.

Tack

- A snaffle bridle, preferably with a simple snaffle bit which has quite a thick, single-jointed, smooth mouthpiece. Either a drop or cavesson noseband is worn (some people prefer to remove the noseband if a lungeing cavesson is fitted). If the reins are not removed they should never be attached to the stirrups or saddle; instead they can be twisted around under the neck and the throatlash put through one of the loops (see opposite).

- A cavesson. This has a padded noseband with three metal rings attached at the front, and a cheek strap. The cavesson is fitted over the bridle and can be buckled either under the chin like a drop noseband, or above the bit like a cavesson noseband. The lunge rein is fastened to the central swivel ring on the noseband. The noseband and cheek strap should be tightened sufficiently to avoid the cheek strap being pulled round to rub the horse's outside eye.

- A lunge rein of about 10m (33ft) long, made of natural fibre or synthetic webbing, with a large loop at one end and a swivel joint attached to a buckle or spring clip at the other.

- Side-reins, which should have a clip at one end and a buckle at the other. There should be a large number of holes at the buckle end so that there is scope for varying the length.

- A roller with rings on either side to which the side-reins can be attached.

- A breast plate to stop the roller or saddle slipping back.

- A saddle, possibly with numnah.

- Boots that are worn on all four legs to prevent damage to them from knocks.

- A lungeing whip with a thong which is long enough to reach the horse.

Lungeing technique

The trainer

The trainer should wear gloves when lungeing so that if the rein is pulled quickly through the hands it will not burn them, and also a hard hat. Spurs should never be worn when lungeing, as they can cause the trainer to trip up.

The trainer who stands correctly will be more efficient and able to react quickly to control the horse who suddenly pulls or turns. In the correct stance:

- The upper body is erect.

- The upper arms hang down with the forearms roughly at right angles to the body.

- The legs are slightly apart.

- Body language is an important aid in the control of the horse on the lunge.

The lunge rein should be held in the hand to which the horse is moving and the whip in the other. The end of the rein is looped so that it can be played out without tangling, and the loops are held in whichever hand the trainer finds it easier to handle the rein efficiently and without getting it tangled.

The lunger's position

The trainer stands at an angle of about 35° to 40° to the horse's forehand, with the horse's head just in front of the trainer's leading shoulder and the trainer in line with the horse's hips. The trainer should concentrate on the movement in the horse's hindquarters rather than the forehand, aiming to drive the horse in a circle. Control over the

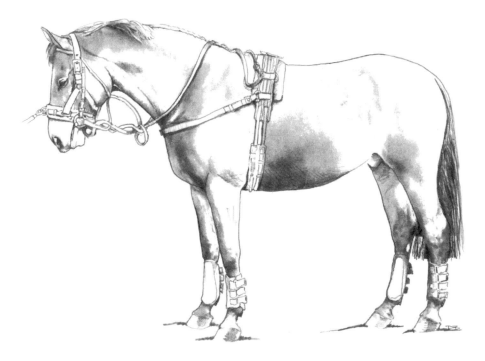

Horse tacked up ready for lungeing. The illustration shows how the reins can be twisted and held by the throatlash.

hindquarters is essential if the trainer is to prevent the horse stopping or turning. The aim should be for the horse, the whip and the rein to form a triangle (see illustration page 134).

The horse should describe a true circle, so the trainer aims to stand on one spot, pivoting around one heel. With the young horse, however, in order to remain in control it might be necessary for the trainer to shorten the rein, move closer to the horse and walk in a small circle. For the horse, though, small circles are a strain: therefore a young horse should never be asked to describe a circle of less than 20m diameter. Only fit, trained horses can be asked to lunge on a smaller circle.

The lungeing aids

The aim is for these to simulate the aids used when riding. The lunge rein is equivalent to the reins; the whip to the legs, and the voice is used in conjunction with both these aids.

The rein should be used by the trainer to maintain a light, consistent contact with the horse, and the aids should be applied with quick movements of the fingers or, if the horse starts to lean on the rein, by giving and restraining, but not by pulling against him.

The whip is used as an aid; the horse should not fear it, but rather he should respect it as he would a schooling whip when being ridden. The horse should therefore be familiarised with it before lungeing and should learn to accept the whip being rubbed along his side and hindquarters.

During lungeing the whip can be applied if needed to make the horse move forward or to increase the activity of the hindquarters. It should be flicked just above the hind fetlocks – but quietly; the trainer should not lurch forward and loosen the rein. Normally the threat of the whip with a swing is sufficient. The whip is also used to keep the horse out on the circle. If he starts to cut corners or to fall in, it can be pointed and, if necessary, flicked in the direction of his shoulder.

The voice is the aid used most frequently, minimising the use of the whip to make the horse go forward and use of the rein to make him slow down. It is also used to soothe and calm the horse and to help him establish a rhythm to his gaits. The effectiveness of the voice is achieved at first in conjunction with the rein and whip aids so that the horse learns that a sharp, quick command 'walk on', 'trot', 'canter', means to move forward, and a low and drawn-out 'whoa', 'wa-alk', 'ter-rot' means to reduce the speed or gait.

The tone of the voice is more important than the actual words used. Lifting the tone of the voice to increase speed or gait and lowering it to decrease speed or gait is usually very effective.

Work on the lunge

It is advisable to start on the rein which the horse finds the easier (usually the left) although he should be worked equally on both reins.

The time spent on the lunge will depend largely on his stage of training, his fitness, and the type of work on the lunge – he could walk for a long time but canter for considerably less. As a general rule, 5 to 10 minutes on each rein is sufficient for a green or unfit horse, and as he gets stronger and more balanced this can be gradually increased to a lesson of about 10 to 15 minutes on each rein.

The horse must never be overworked, otherwise he will lose his enthusiasm and/or might be physically strained.

The novice horse

As soon as a horse is accustomed to wearing a bridle and cavesson, being led from both sides, and has learned to obey the voice aids to walk on and stand still, then he can be lunged.

For the first lesson he should wear the same tack in which he was led – just a snaffle bridle, cavesson and boots. The lunge rein is attached to the central ring on the cavesson.

Assistance

It is advisable for all but the most experienced trainers to use an assistant during these first lessons. The assistant can then lead the horse from the inside of the circle with the lunge rein running through their hands to the trainer in the centre. Once the horse has understood that he is supposed to move around in a circle, the assistant can move closer and closer to the trainer, and if the horse stays out, quietly walk out of the way. The same process should be repeated on the other rein.

It can be dangerous for the assistant to lead the horse from the outside.

The halt

When the horse describes a true circle, he must be taught to halt and walk on when commanded. When being led the horse should have learned that 'whoa' and vibrations on the rein mean 'stop'. These same aids should be applied on the lunge, taking care to control the hindquarters with the whip to prevent the horse from turning in towards the trainer. At first this may require the aid of the assistant.

The horse should halt on the track of the circle (some trainers do ask him to walk in towards them, but this can be detrimental since it encourages the horse to turn in of his own volition). He should not be asked to remain immobile for more than a few seconds. The trainer should then either ask him to walk on again or go out to him (keeping the whip behind the back) to reward with pats, talking and occasional tit-bits.

If the horse does not halt, remember that it may not be through disobedience, but misunderstanding, so be patient. If he persists, work him close to a high hedge or wall (that is unjumpable). If he does not listen to the command to halt/whoa, keep him between the whip and rein to stop him turning in or running down the wall, and direct him towards the wall/high hedge, repeating the command. He will be forced to stop. This method of stopping can, however, cause some horses to panic and rush away from the influence of both the wall and the trainer, so needs to be used with caution. When he does stop, make much of him.

The schedule

There can be no time schedule for the lessons below. The horse should master each one in turn, and should be able to remain calm, relaxed and obedient, before progressing to the next. The early lessons should be performed without side-reins at a free walk and at a working trot. It is best not to canter until the horse is stronger, but if fresh he can be allowed to canter until he settles sufficiently to pay attention.

The stages

Lungeing with a roller. The roller is fitted as on page 118, and the horse is lunged with it in place. The horse has to learn to relax and move freely with this restriction around his back and belly.

Lungeing with a saddle. When the horse is relaxed with a roller it can be replaced by a saddle. At first the stirrups should be removed. In a later lesson they can be run up, and finally before he is backed they can be allowed to hang free for a short time so that the horse gets used to being touched where the rider's legs will be.

Lungeing with side-reins. These are attached to either the roller or the saddle a little above halfway up the horse's sides. To prevent them slipping down, the rings on the roller are the preferred attachments. Before attaching them to the bit, the side-reins are made as long as possible and of equal length, then crossed over at the withers and attached to the Ds on the saddle or roller. The horse is then lunged for a few minutes on both reins to supple up and relax.

The side-reins are then unclipped, and most trainers then attach them directly on to the bit, but some recommend attaching them to the side rings on the cavesson for the first lessons. The horse is then lunged with the side-reins so loose that he cannot feel their effect.

When he works calmly and rhythmically (it might be during that lesson or two or three later), the side-reins can be shortened, but making sure that they both remain of an equal length.

The side-reins should be adjusted to such a length that the horse makes contact with them when he engages his hindquarters, rounds his back and lowers his head. The aim is that as the horse has made the contact himself he will not fear it but will soon start to seek it and to chew gently at the bit.

The side-reins should not be used to pull the horse's head into a particular position, nor should they be so tight that his head comes behind the vertical (see illustration below). The horse's state of balance and way of going must always dictate their length. It is also dangerous for the horse to walk much with the side-reins attached, as they restrict the natural movement of his head and make it more difficult to maintain the correct rhythm of the gait.

As the horse's balance improves he can bring his hind legs further underneath him, his outline becomes shorter and rounder, and the side-reins slacken. This is the time to shorten the side-reins, but never so much that the horse stiffens and resists against them.

Some trainers only use the side-reins for a brief period when familiarising the horse with the contact of the bit, before backing. They prefer to give the horse the freedom both to find his own balance and to stretch forward and down. This also avoids the danger of the horse resisting the contact by either hollowing his back and raising his head (above the bit) or getting overbent and falling behind the contact (behind the bit).

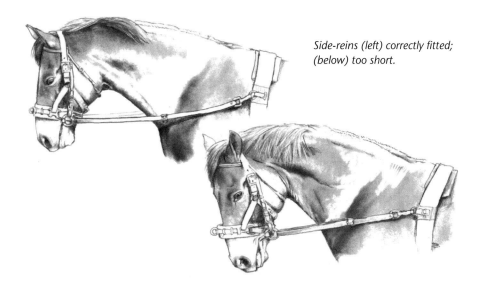

Side-reins (left) correctly fitted; (below) too short.

Straightness on the lunge

Young horses are not straight (see page 141) but lunge work with side-reins helps to reduce crookedness. This is not achieved by shortening the inside rein, which only swings the hindquarters to the outside, throwing the weight on to the inside shoulder and tending to make the horse want to bend to the outside and resist.

If the side-reins are kept at the same length, when the horse places his inside hind leg well under him, which he must do to turn in a circle, his weight will be transferred diagonally towards the outside shoulder. To maintain his balance he will turn his head and neck to the inside. The pressure on the outside rein becomes stronger and the mouth becomes moist on that side, whereas the inside rein becomes looser.

Variations of gait and gaits

The horse can be encouraged to extend the length of his trot stride to do some medium trot, and this is easiest for him if he is driven out of the circle on to a straight line and then returned into a circle in a different place, when he can be returned to the working trot (see illustration below). The canter is introduced when the horse can trot with rhythm, has a willingness to go forward, and moves with a supple, swinging back. Its introduction should be a gradual process, the trainer asking at first for just a few strides on both reins. It is usually advisable to remove the side-reins for early lessons at the canter.

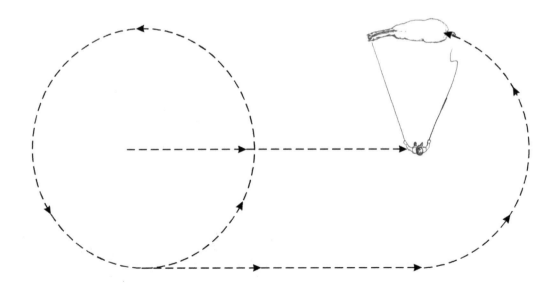

Route of horse and trainer, when the horse lengthens his stride or jumps on the lunge.

It is important for the trainer to recognise if faults are occurring at any of the gaits (e.g. four-time canter). The aim should be to improve the horse's gaits all the time, and to do this the trainer must have a clear picture of what is correct (see Chapter 8).

Backing *(see also Chapter 9)*

A horse who is calm when wearing a saddle and accepts the bit happily at the trot can be backed, but the more time spent on the lunge, the easier it will be for the rider to train the horse. It is, however, advisable for the horse to learn to accept the weight of the rider before he gets too fit and strong. Many trainers therefore back the horse while continuing with training on the lunge: i.e. lunge him for 15 to 20 minutes before he is ridden or alternate days of lungeing with days of riding.

Lungeing over obstacles

Lungeing over poles

This helps to give variety to the work and encourages the young horse to lower his head, round his back and flex his joints. The side-reins are always removed for this work and for all jumping. The horse is first led over the pole, and if he remains relaxed is then lunged at the walk and trot on a circle which is just short of the pole. When he relaxes he can be driven out of the circle and over the pole.

When lungeing over obstacles the trainer must ensure that:

- The horse is presented straight at the pole and does not approach it at an acute angle which would encourage him to run out. This means that the trainer will have to move at right angles to the pole and the horse will no longer describe a circle (see illustration opposite).

- The horse is given as much freedom as possible over the pole and is not restricted by the lunge rein from lowering his head.

- The horse is driven from behind. The trainer should never get in front of him.

- The work is done in equal amounts on both reins.

- The trainer allows the horse to take a number of straight strides upon landing so the horse is not pulled straight back on to a circle.

When the horse walks and trots in a relaxed manner over this single pole in both directions, the exercise can be extended. Poles over which he can be lunged can be scattered around the school or laid in a series either in a straight line or round in a circle. They should be about 1.2–1.35m (4ft–4ft 6in) apart (see also page 202). It is important for them to remain at the correct distance, and if a pole is displaced by the horse the poles should not be attempted again until correctly positioned. Heavy poles help to prevent this occurrence.

Lungeing over raised poles

When the horse trots over the poles in a relaxed manner, maintaining his rhythm and lowering his head, raised poles on blocks can be introduced. The same techniques are used as for poles on the ground (i.e. leading over, using single ones first and progressing to a series).

Lungeing over a fence

Ideally the wing stands of the fence should be low. A pole should be leant against the inside jump stand to prevent the lunge rein being fouled and to act as a wing (see below). With the poles on the ground the horse is led over the fence.

The horse is then lunged over the fence with the poles on the ground. When he does this calmly and without rushing, the end of the pole nearer to the trainer can be raised. When the horse is happy trotting over this, another pole can be added to make a cross bar, and after this a third bar laid along the top, and later a fourth bar to make a parallel.

It is important to make the jumping fun for the horse, and so the progress should be gradual. He should not be asked too much nor should the lessons be too long.

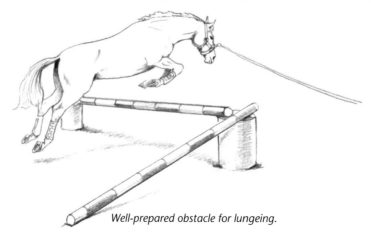

Well-prepared obstacle for lungeing.

More advanced work on the lunge

The main purposes of lungeing more advanced horses are:

- As a means of loosening up horses which, in their preliminary work, stiffen against the weight of the rider.

- As a visual aid to the trainer, who can study from the ground whether the horse is going straight, has sufficient impulsion and suppleness, and that the gaits are true.

- As an aid to collection at the trot and canter. The horse can be gradually brought on to smaller and smaller circles (but never so small that he loses his rhythm or his back stops swinging), while the trainer asks for as much impulsion as possible. Then, while maintaining this collection, the horse is allowed to go back on to a larger circle.

- As an aid to extension at the trot. The horse can be brought into a collected trot, then driven out of the circle on to a straight line, in the same manner as medium trot was asked for in variations of gait on page 113.

- Teaching piaffe (and very occasionally passage) in hand. This work is carried out on straight lines and is described on pages 192–194.

11. The Scales of Training

OUR MODERN TRAINING SYSTEM follows the German Scales of Training, the main aims of which are to be calm, forward and straight. This system is the foundation for the training of riding horses for all aspects of equitation, not just on the flat but when show jumping or going across country. It is the basis for judging dressage both on a National and International level. This system is devised to develop the horse's natural athleticism, to maintain his willingness and gymnastic ability. It enables us to improve submission so we are able to gain influence over the horse's movements without spoiling the quality of his work.

The Scales of Training, often called the building blocks, are:

1. Rhythm

2. Suppleness

3. Contact

4. Impulsion

5. Straightness

6. and eventually Collection

The common denominator of these scales is balance.

Our first priority is to establish the rhythm; with this we can improve the suppleness and from that the contact – each of these building blocks is interlinked with one another. At times we may concentrate more on one of these aspects than another, on a particular day, but we should always return to working on the others.

The Scales of Training are as important to a 3-year-old as they are to an advanced horse and at any point in the training, when a problem arises, we should always return to the basics of training. As the horse develops in his training each of the Scales should develop and improve, relevant to the level the horse has reached.

To enable the horse to develop and improve through the Scales of Training it is essential that the rider also develops their own feel and position, to a balanced, independent, relaxed seat that is able to give effective, unconstrained aids.

The trainability and physical attributes of the horse will affect the progress we can make. It is important that he enjoys his work, so not only should we vary the exercises we choose but also the places where we train; in the school one day, in the field the next.

Each training session should start in walk on a long rein for approximately 10 minutes. This enables the horse to loosen up and warm up his muscles, so he is ready both mentally and physically for his work to progress.

Rhythm

The rhythm should be regular, that is correct for each gait.

- In walk there should be four evenly spaced hoof beats in a marching time.

- In trot there should be two hoof beats, the legs moving in diagonal pairs with a moment of suspension, when all four legs are in the air between each beat.

- In canter there are three hoof beats, with one diagonal pair moving together and a clear moment of suspension when all four legs are off the ground.

The tempo, the speed of the rhythm, should remain consistent whether the horse is going straight or around a corner, lengthening or collecting his strides. The tempo chosen should appear neither too hurried nor so slow as to create dwelling within the stride. To find a regular rhythm and tempo the horse must go willingly forwards and in balance; he must be supple through the back.

Suppleness

Training must develop looseness and suppleness so that the horse uses all his muscles freely and without resistance. He needs to be calm and concentrating so that he can use his energy to its full extent without tension.

Suppleness not only means that he bends equally on both reins but, more importantly, that he uses the muscles of his top line, from the hind legs over the quarters and loins, to the withers and up to his poll. A horse who is supple and working through

Horse going 'on the bit'.

Horse going 'above the bit'.

Horse going 'behind the bit'.

his back works into a round outline, wanting to stretch forwards and down, seeking the rein contact when the rein is lengthened.

Contact

The training of the horse should develop his ability to work from behind over a supple back and neck, stepping energetically to an allowing, elastic rein contact. The horse should accept the contact of the legs and the weight aids so that he steps forwards, with energy, through the whole of his body so that the rider can receive the power from the hind legs in a light rein contact. In this way the horse will establish a round outline and steps, enabling him to produce cadence and impulsion in his trot and canter.

If the horse works with equal power from both hind legs he should work forward to a contact that is even on both sides of the mouth. His mouth should remain still and relaxed, showing no resistance.

The reins should be held with still, quiet, forward-thinking hands. The reins should contain the energy but never pull back and hold the horse into a contact.

Impulsion

Impulsion is the contained power of the horse. Impulsion gives expression to the movement; it can be likened to the gaits he shows when first turned out in a field; this is what we strive to develop when ridden under saddle. The horse needs to place his hind legs more underneath his body, taking more energetic steps which are then contained in the contact of the rein, which with half-halts produces steps that have more expression and cadence.

With a supple back allowing freedom of the shoulders, these steps stay longer in the air but maintain their roundness and the bending of the joints, the action of the hind legs matching those of the forelegs.

Any tightness or resistance will block the energy from getting through, so he must remain supple to allow the connection to be maintained.

It is the skill of the rider to encourage the horse to produce as much energy as possible without the horse hurrying or starting to pull.

Straightness

The long-term aim is to make the horse straight, by this we mean the hind feet step into the tracks of the forefeet both on a straight line and on a circle. The rider should have an even feel on both reins.

We can only make a horse straight when we have established the first three Scales of Training. This is because, like humans, the horse is not born naturally straight; most horses are bent to the left. We can start early to make small corrections but to concentrate on this too much too early will cause the horse to lose expression.

We need to maintain control over the shoulders to improve the straightness; it is important not to overbend the horse in front of the withers, which would enable him to fall out rather than turn where required. Use of the outside rein will enable us to keep the horse's shoulders in front of us.

As the horse becomes straighter his balance will improve and impulsion will develop.

Collection

Collection entails developing the action and strength of the hind limbs; the horse lowers the quarters and hocks so that he can take more weight behind, this enables him to use his strength to its full potential. The more weight he takes behind, the lighter and freer are the shoulders, and the more athletic he becomes. This makes the horse easier to ride and control, more powerful but manoeuvrable.

When the horse is first ridden his weight will be carried more on the forehand and he will find it hard to respond quickly to the rider's aids. He will tend to run faster when asked to lengthen his strides, find it difficult to stop quickly and will often rely on the rider's hands to maintain or regain his balance.

Throughout his training his collection will develop and change as he builds strength and engagement. Even a Novice test will require a greater amount of engagement of the hindquarters than a Preliminary test to enable the horse to do the more difficult movements, e.g.10m circles in trot. At each level of dressage the collection required will increase until the horse reaches Grand Prix level when he will 'trot on the spot' in piaffe or turn around on the spot in a canter pirouette. This engagement is equally important when show jumping or jumping cross-country when the strength and engagement of the hind legs will be needed to make a greater effort over larger fences and sharper turns.

Summary

In the basic, initial training we do not ask for too high a standard of any of the Scales of Training, each being developed progressively. If the training is rushed, without enough attention to any of the basics, we will create tension and resistance, with a horse who will never be able to fulfil his potential. In the same way, if we do not push him, sometimes a little out of his comfort zone, he will not progress. Whenever a problem arises we should always go back and reconfirm the basics.

By training the horse using the Scales of Training, the horse will develop so that he will be able to progress to whichever discipline he has most talent for.

When there is rhythm, suppleness, contact, impulsion, straightness and collection, relevant to the stage of training, the way of going will be good.

12. Training Principles for Ridden Work

A HORSE WHO HAS COMPLETED THE TRAINING covered in Chapter 9 should be moving freely forward, calmly and confidently beginning to understand the basic aids of the rider. In order for the horse to develop and improve, his trainer/rider needs to understand the essential training principles as set out in Chapter 11, The Scales of Training.

The basic training of the horse:

- Stimulates his willingness to go forward.

- Develops his natural abilities.

- Strengthens his physique.

- Makes him more supple and gymnastic.

- Increases his stamina.

- Gives the rider more control.

General principles

The following are important:

- **Avoidance of short cuts.** Training requires time, effort and patience. Short cuts, such as the use of gadgets, should be avoided as these develop resistances and create their own problems.

- **Rate of progress.** Training cannot be conducted to a timescale; it must be dependent on the progress made. The rate of progress will vary according to the ability and temperament of the horse and the rider. Although the trainer plans a programme for progressive training, it must be sufficiently flexible to suit the individual characteristics of the horse being trained.

- **Use of reward and punishment.** The following system of training uses rewards and punishments, but no force, to teach the acceptance of the aids and obedience to the rider. The amount of reward and punishment will vary according to the character of the horse. Hot-blooded, high-spirited horses usually need more rewards than lazy horses, who may benefit from occasional reprimands. The trainer must analyse the character of the horse and apply the appropriate discipline. In all cases persuasion is recommended as being more effective than coercion. A frightened horse is too tense to learn. The aim must be willing cooperation obtained by rational and tactful methods, but at the same time there must never be any doubt as to who is in command; if authority and respect are lost, training stops.

Qualities of the trainer/rider

Since it is the rider who trains the horse it will be assumed throughout this chapter that the trainer is the rider.

A good trainer has the following qualities:

- Ability to make the horse understand. If the horse does not obey, the trainer must consider whether the horse understood the instructions given. Before blaming the horse, the trainer should give due consideration to the aids and methods used.

  NB If a good basic position has been established by the trainer the aids can be given more clearly.

- An understanding of the general nature of a horse and an ability to adapt the approach according to the temperament and individual characteristics of the horse being trained.

- Patience and persistence.

- Temper must always be controlled.

- An air of calm authority when with the horse: ensuring that all movements are quiet and deliberate.

- Tolerance of playful high spirits in a young horse, but firmness in the face of wilful disobedience.

- A good sense of rhythm.

- A sufficient knowledge of horsemastership in order to ensure that the horse is being well cared for and suitably fed.

Warming up and cooling down

Warming up

Throughout training it is necessary to warm the horse up prior to any work session. This loosening of the muscles is essential if the horse is expected to be able to work in a supple, compliant way, in both body and mind. No athlete can have a successful training or competitive session if he has not loosened up effectively, so that the muscles are warm, flexible and ready for further demands made on them.

The way in which a horse is warmed up may ultimately be modified a little to suit each individual horse and rider. However, the basic criteria are that:

- The horse is loosened systematically so that his muscles are relaxed and warm and ready for further work.

- The horse is mentally calm and attuned to the rider so that more demanding work can begin.

- The horse is physically and mentally able to accept and respond in the best way, to the discipline of the rider.

Warming up will usually include some or all of the following guidelines:

- Walk the horse on loose or long reins in a quiet area for 5 or 10 minutes.

- Walk the horse quietly up the road or similar, with or without other horses.

- The horse may be walked on a horse-walker for 5 to 10 minutes prior to work.

- Lungeing can be used as a means of loosening and warming up but this should be in a long outline without the demands of short side-reins.

- The horse may be walked on a contact and moved through some simple lateral movements (leg yield, shoulder-fore, quarters-in) to begin to supple him.

- Some rising trot may follow any of the above walk work. The trot should be forward on fairly easy (long) reins, encouraging the horse to work confidently forward to seek the contact through a swinging back and a supple, loose frame.

- The horse may be worked quite forward and 'down' at this stage – this must never be confused with pushing the horse out of balance and onto his forehand, where the shoulders become more restricted and loaded. In this forward trot, the gait should be swinging without being hurried and the horse should show a looseness and freedom in his early connection from leg to hand.

- The canter may be used in the same way and the rider may choose to take a slightly lighter seat in the early canter to encourage the horse to start 'letting go' through his muscles, particularly those in his back.

- The time taken to loosen and warm the horse up will vary from horse to horse.

- Some young horses may take a long time to learn to 'let go'. Some older horses take longer to loosen than they did when they were younger.

- The relaxation of the mind is as important as that of the body, but finding the key can sometimes be difficult.

- An inattentive, anxious horse must be approached in whatever way ultimately achieves relaxation. There are no right or wrong answers here as long as the interests of the horse are paramount.

Cooling down

The period immediately after a demanding work session is as important as the warming up. After (ideally) a satisfactory moment on which to finish the work, the horse should be progressively cooled down.

- Straight after the last piece of demanding work, the horse may be encouraged to take the reins forward and down in either trot or canter.

- This is similar to the working-in practice. The horse is encouraged to stretch forward and down, thus alleviating the demands that have been made on the muscles, particularly in the hindquarters and back.

- The horse should not lose balance and quicken, falling onto his forehand; he should just take the rein forward and down while maintaining a balanced, swinging, rhythmical gait with active engagement of the hind legs.

- The horse may then be walked for several minutes to allow him to completely relax and dry off (if sweating) before returning to the stable.

- It is very important that the muscles should not be allowed to get cold. Depending on the time of year and the weather, the horse should be walked off, perhaps in a quarter sheet or anti-sweat sheet.

- On returning to the stable he should be washed or sponged down, and/or brushed off and rugged according to his needs.

- It is as important that rider's own condition is not neglected after a work session. For example, it is important to put on a coat or waistcoat immediately after a work session in order to avoid becoming chilled.

13. Preparatory Training of the Ridden Horse

THE PREPARATORY STAGE OF TRAINING (lasting 4 to 12 months, depending on the ability of the horse and trainer) aims to produce a horse who:

- Has fine, regular and unhurried gaits.

- Is calm, relaxed and obedient to the aids of the rider.

- Shows a good natural outline, balance and rhythm.

- Moves freely forward, without collection, but with active hindquarters.

- Accepts the bit willingly, without tension or resistance.

- Remains straight when moving on straight lines and bent correctly when moving on curved lines.

- Executes transitions smoothly and remains still when halted.

- Is a pleasure to ride in the school and out of doors.

The work should include:

- Work on the flat.

- Gymnastic jumping exercises.

- Riding out, including hill work.

Work on the flat

Pattern of work. It is best to start at the rising trot on the horse's easier rein and then to change to the more difficult rein. The first part of the work is aimed at loosening up and relaxing the horse by working him down. All the work should be on both reins, and approximately equal time should be spent on each rein.

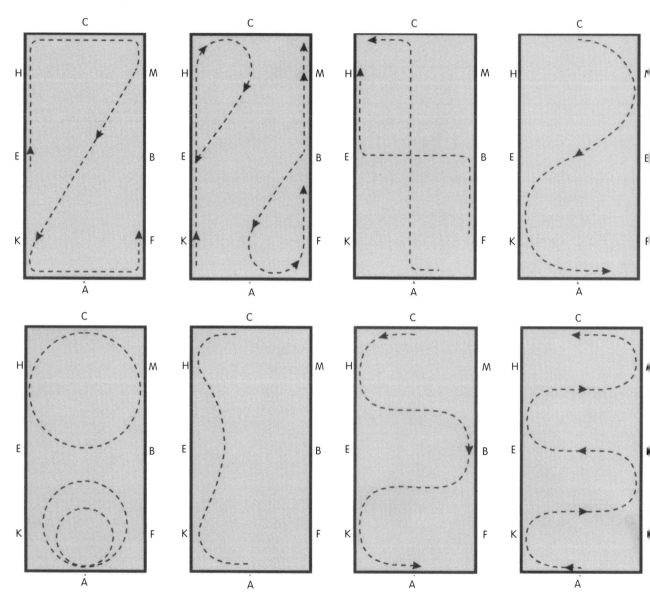

Figures used during work on the flat. Top row: methods of changing the rein. Bottom row, from left to right: 20m, 15m and 10m circles; shallow loop (5m); three-loop serpentine; four-loop serpentine.

Frequent rest periods at the walk on a long rein are needed, and it is wise to finish on a good note performing a movement that the horse can do well.

When the horse trots with lively steps and a relaxed, swinging back he should begin to present a degree of roundness in his outline, with the poll at the highest point of his neck. When he has reached this stage he is ready for the sitting trot.

148

Duration. Half an hour to 50 minutes, or two sessions of 30 minutes are average sessions, but it depends greatly on the strength and temperament of the individual horse.

The figures

From this early stage of training it is important to get into the discipline of executing accurate figures.

The circles should be round, the straight lines straight, and the horse taken as deep into the corners as is possible without losing impulsion, rhythm, correct bend and the willingness to go forward.

The circles should be limited to 20m in diameter, the half-circles to 15m in diameter, and the loops of a serpentine to 12m in diameter.

The gaits

These should be limited to a free walk on a long rein, the medium walk, a working trot and working canter (see Chapter 8). When the horse is ready to canter he must learn to strike off on the correct leg. The easiest position for this is either when on a circle, or when going into the short side of the school. If he strikes off on the wrong leg he should not be made to halt – which he might regard as a form of punishment – but just to trot, and the strike-off should be tried again. If for any reason the horse when asked to canter goes into a fast trot, he should not be allowed to strike off until a calm, relaxed working trot has been established. Cantering is difficult for a young horse, especially on the circle, and should not be continued for too long. Many young horses find it easier to canter with their backs rounded and relaxed if the trainer is in a jumping position with the seat bones just out of the saddle.

The transitions

These should be progressive: i.e. not directly from canter to walk, but through trot, similarly with upward transitions. In the early stages of training, the manner in which a transition is executed is more important than its achievement at a given marker.

Transitions should be carried out smoothly but not abruptly. If the horse does not respond, ask again and again if necessary, so that the aids are repetitive, not continuous. For a transition to be satisfactory, the horse must be balanced as he goes into it, and must have sufficient impulsion. The rhythm of the gait should be maintained up to the moment that the gait is changed, or the horse is halted, and should be established in the new gait as soon as possible.

- Upward transitions (page 100). It is essential for the rider to prepare the young horse for an upward transition and, in particular, to develop enough impulsion to enable the horse to obey without throwing his head in the air or hollowing his back.

- Downward transitions (pages 102–103). These must be ridden forward, the trainer maintaining a correct seat and using a restraining but allowing hand. (Pulling backwards on the reins will create resistances and stiffen the horse's back.) In the early stages it is helpful to use the voice to avoid having to pull on the reins.

Movements

These should be limited to an understanding of the half-halt, the halt, and the turn on the forehand. (For a full explanation of the turn on the forehand, see pages 171–172.)

The half-halt (see also page 102)

This is a hardly visible, moderated version of the halt, which:

1. Increases the attention and balance of the horse.

2. Helps to engage the hindquarters, to generate impulsion, and to lighten the forehand.

3. Warns the horse that the rider is about to ask something of him. To be effective, the rider must, as in all the work, get the horse to think forward: i.e. the driving aids are more important than the restraining aids. The seat and leg aids are applied to produce more activity in the hindquarters, which should have repercussions on other muscles in the horse's body (i.e. the muscles are coordinated, so the aids go 'through' and are not isolated to the hindquarters). To stop the driving aids simply increasing the horse's speed, the rein or reins momentarily restrain. This results in the increased energy and attention produced by the driving aids being contained within the horse, to result in 1. and 2. above.

If the half-halt is to be effective, the horse's back must be relaxed and swinging to enable the aids to go 'through' and allow the back to perform its function of acting as a connecting link between the forehand and the hindquarters. If the back is tense, the rein aids cannot go 'through' and the tendency will be for the horse to raise his head, hollow his back and lose the engaging effect of the half-halt.

After applying the rein aid the rider then gives momentarily with the hands so that the horse learns to hold himself together and does not rely for support on the reins. At the intermediate stage the rider should aim to 'hold' the horse with seat and leg aids without reliance on the reins.

The half-halt becomes more important as training progresses, but the young horse should be gradually introduced to the aids and should learn to accept them correctly.

The halt (see also page 103)

It is important from the beginning of the ridden work, for the novice horse to be taught to stand still when halted. Initially he should be halted largely through use of the voice and with a light contact on the bit; for a second or two he should not move his legs or head. The novice horse should not be asked to stand still for too long; about three seconds is enough. Too much importance should not be attached to the novice horse standing square. One hind leg is often left behind a little and it is better for the rider to remain still, rather than trying to correct the fault, which usually disappears as the horse becomes more supple and engaged. Not until the horse readily accepts the bit and is really going forward will he be able to bring his hind legs sufficiently under him to establish his balance and to stand with his weight equally adjusted over all four legs.

Gymnastic jumping exercises

These are discussed in detail in Chapter 17.

As soon as the horse has learned to accept the bit, and to walk, trot, and canter without excitement, he should receive elementary jumping lessons. They are valuable in teaching the horse to use himself athletically, thereby strengthening his muscles and making him both supple and mentally alert. They can be given about twice a week, on good going.

At this novice stage the fences should be used to give a horse confidence and should never be too large. Work up from little fences to about 1m (3ft 3in) in height, with a maximum of 1.5m (5ft) spread. Grids with accurately measured distances between the obstacles are initially the most valuable.

Riding out

It is essential to keep a young horse's interest. He will soon tire of school work if he is weak and finds it an effort. Riding out, especially hill work, will help to develop his muscles as well as providing him with the variety which will be mentally refreshing. Frequent riding out is, therefore, advisable, but the objects of training can still be kept in mind. Hacking across fields, over undulating ground, along lanes, need not be time off but another opportunity to develop the objectives of basic training.

In this outside work, control is vital. If it is lost the horse and rider will be frightened, so a trainer must gauge how much can be asked of the pupil. A nervous horse should not be asked to meet heavy traffic or other new, frightening experiences (e.g. farm machinery) without the company of another more reliable horse. If going for a canter the trainer should sense when the horse is showing signs of 'coming to the boil', and reduce the speed before risking loss of control; then the occasional gallop can be enjoyed with safety.

Visits to horse shows, where a young horse can get used to crowds, other horses and strange sights, are a useful experience. Towards the end of this stage of training, a day or two out with the local hunt can be beneficial, especially for potential eventers or jumpers who need to get accustomed to different obstacles, and for lazy horses to develop impulsion.

After riding out, the trainer should examine the horse in the stable for possible injury and in order to assess his general condition.

# 14. General Principles of Training the Dressage Horse

THE WORD 'DRESSAGE' CAN BE INTERPRETED IN MANY WAYS. Taken from the French *'dresseur'*, meaning 'trainer', it can be thought of as improving and developing a horse's natural physique, beauty and movement, whilst working in harmony with his rider. Competition dressage has evolved from this ethos. Even at the most basic level, riders are judged on the presentation of their horse's training, highlighting that they are safeguarding the purity of the gaits and progressing in accordance with the Scales of Training (see Chapter 11). Riders, trainers and judges all have a responsibility to safeguard these principles.

In this chapter the aim is to explain how a raw 3-year-old is trained to mature into a Grand Prix dressage horse. This is a long, slow process. With no hold ups or mishaps a talented horse can learn all the movements by the time he reaches 8 years of age. It will take an exceptional horse and rider to be able to present a Grand Prix test at 9 years old, most achieving this stage at 10 and not reaching their peak in competition until they are around 14. Only a small minority of horses who set out on this journey will have the physical and mental ability to reach Grand Prix. However, whatever a horse's future career, a sound foundation in dressage will make him physically stronger and give him an understanding of the basic aids. He will thus be more pleasurable to ride. Dressage is basic education for every horse: whether his intended career is reining, polo, racing, endurance or one of the Olympic disciplines a sound foundation in dressage will always be of benefit.

Starting the young horse

The backing and early training process of a young horse is dealt with elsewhere in this book (see Chapter 9), but there are some important safeguards that apply to all horses. The young horse's mouth must be well looked after. Resistance to the bit is severely penalised in dressage, for example problems such as drawing the tongue back or over the bit are often the result of poorly fitting tack or rough handling. Young horses should have their mouths thoroughly checked by a qualified equine dentist before being introduced to the bit. The trainer should be aware that at this age (3–4 years old), the horse's teeth are changing and care should be taken to avoid him getting sore.

Lungeing

The lungeing process, with the correct use of side-reins, will train the young horse to work forward to the bit and to look for the contact. It will also build his strength, particularly of his back muscles. It introduces him to the voice aids and he learns to go forward from the whip. Lungeing will give him confidence in his trainer and he will develop a bond and trust in human contact.

In order to safeguard the purity of the gaits of a dressage horse when lungeing, side-reins should never artificially shorten the horse's neck. This is particularly important in the walk; the horse must take the bit forward using his whole body. Good footing and large circles are also important; the trot should be balanced and consistent in the rhythm, the canter used judiciously and in a clear three-beat rhythm. Patient trainers will allow their 3-year-olds two to three months of preparatory work to develop their strength before being backed.

Backing

The backing process (see Chapter 9) is much the same for all horses, although the facilities available are a factor. It is essential that the rider is able to stay in balance and does not pull the horse's mouth about. The horse must learn to go forwards and even at this stage he should be encouraged to look for an elastic contact. It is preferable to work young horses in either an eggbutt or loose-ring jointed snaffle which is not too thick. Many have quite small mouths and find a thick bit uncomfortable. The width of the bit should also be correct. It might be useful to change to a bit with a lozenge later on in the training, but for this early work it is important for the horse to be comfortable with the bit but not to play with it too much.

Early ridden work

The early ridden work should involve 'socialising' the youngster. He must learn to deal with other horses in the school, he must also learn to work on his own and not to get upset and distracted by others coming and going. With a 3-year-old between 15 and 30 minutes in the school three to four times a week is ample. Time in between or preferably in addition should be spent loose in the field, hacking in a safe environment with another horse or on a horse-walker. He has to work to develop, but it should not be intense. If he does get fresh, some lungeing or a day in the field is better than trying to tire him out under saddle.

In the school we are working to develop his rhythm and his confidence. Most of the training will be in working trot rising; use big circles, easy turns and don't ride too deep into the corners at this stage. Walk on a contact should be for brief periods before and after a transition, otherwise ride walk on a long rein, provided it is safe to do so, making him understand that he must go forwards by himself.

Do not fall into the trap of using too much leg; it is very easy to make a horse insensitive to the leg by using it constantly.

Canter is where most young horses can experience difficulties with their balance. Make sure that the going is suitable and that you have enough space. Use your voice and leg to get him to strike off from a balanced trot; don't worry if he runs off in trot to begin with. Ask coming into the first corner of the short side. If he strikes off incorrectly do not pull him up immediately but let him canter a few strides before returning quietly to trot and asking again. He must understand that he can go forward. A couple of circuits of the school are enough at this stage.

The 4-year-old

When your youngster comes into his fourth year he should have developed a basic understanding of working trot and canter, medium and free walk. He should know how to turn and to stop and go. In this second period of training we start to ride more transitions, mostly from walk to trot and back again, working on his reactions to the aids and developing his ability to engage his hind legs. The strength of his back will determine whether he is ready to work in sitting trot. When sitting, you must be competent enough to do so with a relaxed, supple seat so that your hips and lower back absorb the movement without bumping. If the horse tightens up and resists you, sitting trot is going to have a negative effect on his training. Go rising again and wait until he is stronger.

The outline at this stage should be fairly 'horizontal' with the neck stretching down and forwards to the bit. His back should be round and swinging and his hind legs should step under his body. His mouth should be soft and quiet with a moderate amount of saliva lubricating the bit. He should already be giving the impression of a supple athlete.

How quickly he progresses now is a very individual matter. Careful observation must be made of his physical and mental health. A loss of enthusiasm and sparkle, a little heat in a joint, resistance to the aids, are all signs that it is time to back off. A few days rest in the field, some hacking or making the work more basic again will prevent a little 'niggle' developing into problem.

By the end of his fourth year he should understand the canter strike-off on either lead, be able to carry out some basic leg yielding in trot, know how to halt and remain still, and how to move off from a halt. He should be fairly straight, and able to bend sufficiently in the direction in which he is moving on large circles and easy turns. He must accept the bit and work willingly forward, without tension, from light leg aids. He should be confident in a variety of situations and may even have had his first show outing, but only if he is mature enough to handle it.

The 5-year-old

The 5-year-old horse requires the trainer to understand his individual strengths and weaknesses. A precocious 5-year-old with a natural ability in canter may be able to learn flying changes, but the same horse may find medium trot very difficult. Some find the lateral work effortless; others get upset by it. The art is to be able to make progress and keep the horse confident. Normally, we work to develop the medium trot and canter at this stage. It can be productive to teach the horse to make transitions between a medium and a working gait that is approaching collection. Ask for only a few medium strides then ask the horse to return to a working gait before he loses balance; once he responds you can then ask him to lengthen again. This keeps the horse thinking forward and means that he is not jarring his legs, which can happen if he loses balance and coordination in the medium work. Some horses have big extensions naturally; others have to develop it. Extended trots should only be ridden on good going and on straight lines and not too often. Protect your young horse's soundness at all costs.

You should also by now be making some progress with his understanding of lateral work. Leg yielding is the least complicated exercise, to which he should have been introduced as a 4-year-old. You can now ask him to leg yield in walk and trot across the school and also to change from one direction to the other. He should keep the rhythm and show only a small flexion at the poll away from the direction in which he is moving. Once he is comfortable with this he can be introduced to shoulder-in. It is useful to 'show the way' in lateral work by starting out in walk; this allows the horse to understand without losing balance. To get into shoulder-in, keep the bend coming out of a corner and ride the first step of a 10m circle. Once the forehand is off the track, use your inside leg to move the horse sideways down the track. Think of lining up his inside hip, your inside seat bone and his outside shoulder. His inside hind leg should step under his body;

he should give the illusion of bend in his body and that same amount of bend should continue along his neck.

Canter work should include counter-canter at this stage. Counter-canter is the most useful exercise for developing obedience, suppleness, straightness and collection and remains valuable even for Grand Prix horses. Start with gentle loops, 3m in from the track and progress to changing the rein and being able to canter round the short side of the arena. Never punish a young horse for offering a flying change at this point – you will be only too happy for him to show this talent later. If he breaks or changes, calmly balance him in trot and then ride a curved line so that he is bent in the direction to strike off on the lead that you want.

Canter to walk transitions and walk to canter should be introduced; initially, the transitions can be progressive, i.e. through a step or two of trot. This is where your aids and timing must be clear; you are teaching him a language and must be consistent.

Once your horse is secure in counter-canter, and if he can also 'change gear' easily between medium and a more 'collected' working canter, then he is ready to do flying changes. Some horses pick these up effortlessly; others can take, literally, a couple of years! It is all to do with the adjustability of the canter and the feel and experience of the rider. Some horses get quite upset during this process; others accept changes really easily. Experienced riders will recognise a moment in the horse's canter where they feel they have the 'right quality' to ask for a change. The best place is on the short diagonal; keep the horse's shoulders from falling in to the new lead and use the same aid as you would for a strike-off on the new lead. Most likely nothing will happen and you will need to reinforce the aid a little stronger. Sometimes horses will go disunited, sometimes they will buck; just work quietly with the individual horse's reactions. If you don't achieve a correct change in the first few attempts, leave them alone for a few weeks and go back to improving the canter.

Rather like teenagers, 5-year-olds will often try to push the boundaries. They are often keen to test their strength and your resolve. A big, strong Warmblood can present you with some tricky situations. Always try to be fair and avoid getting into a situation where he may get the upper hand. He must go where he is asked and when he is asked, so don't expect him on his own, for example, to go past a new and frightening object when you are on concrete. He may slip and fall, injuring you both, so get another more experienced horse to give you a lead, then go past a few times on your own. This is where your training in shoulder-in will really be of benefit.

Sometimes horses at this age experience pain in their mouths, through changing teeth, or they can feel back pain, etc. Always check out that there are no medical reasons for continued resistance.

Five-year-olds also need to be further 'socialised'. It is a good idea to take them for short trips in your horsebox or trailer. Hire an arena and get the horse used to working in new surroundings when it is quiet. Get permission from a show organiser to bring him along to a competition just to train then, if he is upset, you don't have the pressure of a competition and can spend the time and energy getting him properly relaxed. If all goes to plan then he should be ready to do some easy tests.

In competition it is important that he has a good experience, so ride him to improve his training for the future. It is tempting to try to prevent green mistakes by restricting the horse's natural movement and 'fixing him in a frame', but he must react to your leg and learn that he cannot ignore you when in the competition arena.

The 6-year-old

By the age of 6 your horse should be well on in his education. Travers and half-passes on easy lines should be introduced; again you can start in walk before moving on into trot. Some horses find half-pass in canter easier as they already have a natural bend over the leading leg. Walk pirouettes also need to be mastered. You will find the horse is developing more strength, muscle and collection. It is now a question of making everything secure and gaining confidence. The changes should now be more established; you might not have them ready for public viewing but the horse should now understand them.

There is a saying that you should train the horse slowly for the first two years and then he will train quickly for the rest. You should now start to reap the benefits of your patience. The next few years will be spent developing and improving the work that you have taught him so far.

More advanced work

Piaffe and passage

The young horse will, hopefully, by now have given you some indication of whether he has a talent for piaffe and passage. He may have got excited, put his tail in the air and elevated his stride into passage, or, on being restrained, he may have shown you some piaffe steps. If he does, see if you can sustain this for a few extra steps to sow the seeds for the future.

There are many ways to teach piaffe, from the ground or under saddle. Your method will depend on your situation and facilities. You do need expert guidance if you have not done this before. One option, which works for some horses (especially if you don't have access to a fenced school), is to teach them piaffe, mounted, from collected walk. It helps in the early stages to have someone on the ground with a whip to touch the horse to get the appropriate reaction. This person must have experience and be able to keep themselves safe. They must also have good timing and understanding to make sure that the rider is not bucked off or, worse still, that the horse becomes frightened and runs back, perhaps falling over backwards. Lots of praise, including offering sugar or mints is necessary, so that the horse enjoys this work.

Passage is developed from the piaffe, using a slow trot encouraging suspension and elevation. Again make sure that the horse gradually builds his strength and fitness with this work.

Advances in canter

More advanced canter work includes building the strength and collection in the canter to develop canter pirouettes. The horse should be able to canter almost on the spot with ease on a straight line. Then you can think about bending him and doing some quarters-in on a circle before making some quarter pirouette steps. Gradually build this up and he will then be able to perform large, full pirouettes of six to eight strides with ease.

You can then build up the flying changes so that you can ask for them anywhere in the school, including changing into counter-canter. The tempi changes such as the fours, threes and twos will develop easily enough. Priority should be given to the 'throughness' and correctness of the rhythm and then the straightness. Some horses get upset or overexcited with tempi changes, but be patient and vary the exercise. Only ever ask for a change when the canter is active and balanced and the horse is listening to you. Some horses get resistant to the leg in the changes, so it is important here that you keep contact with your lower leg; don't teach the horse that you will back off if he pushes against you.

The one-time changes require quick reactions from the rider and for the horse to be in an active, sharp, collected canter. To begin with just ask for two; if those are achieved, do two more and so on. When asking for three or more, you don't have time to think 'has he changed?', just get into the rhythm. The aids are the same as for a strike-off; you just make them smaller and keep asking. Do not fall into the trap of throwing yourself from side to side. Remember quality is more important than quantity with one-time changes.

From this stage, to reach Grand Prix it is just a question of linking all the work together and practising each component of the test until the horse can flow from one movement to the next.

The dressage horse, like the gymnast, needs to practise and develop his strength. He needs to be trained at least four times a week and to go hacking or do something easy in between. He will need a complete break each year but until the work is established he will spend a lot of time schooling. Keep him sweet with time in the field and/or, if facilities allow, hacking.

The finished article of a Grand Prix dressage horse comes from years of patient and dedicated training, coupled with excellent and meticulous stable management. The reward lies in producing a horse who is a pleasure to ride and who thoroughly enjoys working with his rider.

15. Intermediate Training of the Ridden Horse

THE INTERMEDIATE STAGE is a continuation of the preparatory stage, further developing the objectives of training but with increasing emphasis being placed on collection.

Collection

Collection becomes an important objective at this stage, but it is only possible to develop if the trainer maintains and improves the other objectives:

- Rhythm

- Suppleness

- Contact

- Impulsion

- Straightness

as discussed in Chapter 11 The Scales of Training.

Benefits of collection

- The development and improvement of the horse's balance.

- The engagement and lowering of his hindquarters, which will lighten and make his forehand more mobile. This enables the strides to become longer or higher, as desired.

- The horse will develop more ease and self-carriage in his work, which will make him more pleasant to ride.

Developing impulsion and carrying capacity (the ability to take weight onto the hindquarters).

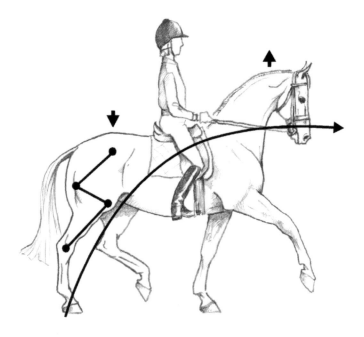

The horse should become more manoeuvrable, more able to generate the power to extend his gaits, carry out dressage movements, and jump fences.

To collect

Collection is achieved by greater engagement of the hindquarters, and not a slowing down to produce trudging, inactive steps. When asking the horse to shorten and heighten his strides into collection, impulsion must be maintained, or even increased.

The major aids for collection are half-halts, increasingly small circles, serpentines, variations within a gait, smooth, direct downward and upward transitions, and lateral movements.

General work on the flat

The work first entails lengthening and loosening up the muscles, then flexing them into collection. When asking the horse for an effort, the trainer must first be certain of the intended aims and also that the horse is physically and mentally ready for the cooperation needed. If problems arise, revert to the basic principle of 'straighten your horse and ride him forward', as so many difficulties arise from loss of impulsion and crookedness.

The work must continue to be progressive, using the figures and movements discussed in this chapter to improve the objectives of training. Thus from merely learning to remain immobile the horse can be taught to halt square and rein-back; from the easiest lateral work of the turn on the forehand and leg yielding progress to the shoulder-in and half-pass; and from canter work in counter-canter and use of simple changes, progress to flying changes.

Not only should the movements tackled be progressive but also the manner in which they are performed. Thus the trainer will progress from achieving just a few steps of a movement to quite lengthy phases of the movement; from performing, for example, shoulder-in with little collection finishing on a circle, to shoulder-in down the length of the school in greater collection, finishing with the horse being straightened back on the track; from riding half-pass with very little bend and very much forward, to asking for a good deal of bend and sideways movement. Although trainers should keep in mind how Grand Prix horses perform movements, they must realise that it takes considerable muscular power and suppleness to perform them this way. They can only be developed with progressive work. Also, few eventers or show jumpers would be able, or need, to develop the collection required for accurate Grand Prix dressage movements.

The figures

The trainer can gradually reduce the sizes of the circles as more collection is achieved to 10m diameter, and half-circles of 6m diameter. The circles for the medium trot and medium canter should not be smaller than 20m diameter, and the extended canter should be ridden along straight tracks.

Serpentines are an excellent suppling exercise; the size of the loops can be gradually reduced. The serpentine can be used in trot, and in canter with simple changes on the centre line, or some counter-canter loops. For other useful movements see page 148.

Transitions

As long as they are performed correctly, frequent transitions from one gait to another, and transitions within the gait, help to achieve the objectives of training.

When working, the trainer can gradually increase the degree of collection in the horse and can alternate this successively with the medium and extended gaits.

Transitions of two levels up – e.g. halt to trot, walk to canter – can be executed together with similar downward transitions.

The transitions should be made more quickly and less progressively than in the preliminary stage.

Aims

- To show a clear transition.

- To be quick, but smooth and not abrupt.

- To maintain the rhythm of the gait up to the moment that the gait is changed, or the horse halts.

- For the new gait to be true and to show lively impulsion.

- For the horse to remain 'on the bit', light in hand, and calm.

- To remain balanced and 'on the bit'.

The halt *(see also page 103)*

Aims

At the halt in the preliminary stage the horse was first and foremost immobile, but not necessarily four-square. Now the aims should be:

- To distribute the weight evenly on all four legs which are pairs abreast of each other (a square halt).

A good, square halt, with the horse remaining 'on the bit'.

- To hold the neck so that the poll is the highest point and the head is slightly in front of the vertical.

- To remain 'on the bit' and maintain a supple jaw.

- To remain motionless, but attentive, and ready to move off at the wish of the rider.

Execution

More of the horse's weight has to be transferred to his hindquarters by increasing the action of the rider's seat and legs, which should drive the horse towards a more and more restraining but allowing hand. By this intermediate stage the halt should be almost instantaneous, but not abrupt.

The rein-back

The horse moves backwards, raising and setting down his legs in almost diagonal pairs.

Aims

- To lift the feet off the ground so that the limbs are not dragged.

- To remain straight.

- To step back in a deliberate rhythm.

- To make all the steps the same length.

- To move forward without halting when asked.

The rein-back.

Execution

The rein-back should not be asked for before the horse has become reasonably supple, flexible in his joints, and off his forehand, otherwise he will find it difficult and will have to be pulled back, which usually leads to a hollowing of the back and further resistances. If the horse does not respond in spite of being ready to learn to rein-back, the rider must not pull him back, but should push him onto a stronger contact.

The stages

- Practise frequent smooth transitions to the halt, with the horse standing four-square and remaining on the bit.

- After a further good halt, apply the aids to move forward but with the hands restraining the forward movement. As the horse steps back, lighten the contact as a reward, but still keep him on the bit.

- One or two steps are sufficient in the early stages.

- After stepping back, the horse should walk forward without hesitation when asked to do so.

- The rider must control each backward step and vary the number asked for.

The rider

- Establishes a square halt and takes care that the horse remains on the bit.

- Eases the weight in the saddle by putting more weight into the stirrups and on the thighs.

- Applies the legs just behind the girth.

- Prevents the consequent inclination to move forward by restraining aids on the reins.

- Releases the pressure on the reins as soon as the horse steps back. It is essential that the rider does not pull backwards on the reins as the horse will then resist or run back stiffly. The horse must also be kept straight by appropriate use of the rider's legs and, if necessary, the reins.

The counter-canter

The rider asks the horse to travel in the opposite direction to that of the leading leg and bend, so that when on a curve to the left the horse canters with the right lead and vice versa.

Aims

- To maintain the bend to the leading leg so that the horse looks to the outside of the curve.

- To keep the hindquarters from swinging to the outside of the curve.

- To maintain the rhythm and balance.

Execution

The rider should only ask according to the suppleness and collection of the horse and should always bear in mind that the conformation of the horse does not allow him to be bent to the line of the circle. The early lessons can consist of loops off a straight line. Then progress, as the aims set about above are maintained, to circles and serpentines.

Benefits

- An important suppling and balancing exercise and improves straightness.

- Encourages the engagement of the hindquarters if carried out correctly.

- Can be of use when teaching flying changes.

The rider

- Uses the same aids as for the canter, maintaining the position towards the leading leg so that, for example, position left is maintained when in counter-canter around a right turn. At first it may be necessary to hold this position more strongly, with the legs definitely applied and the weight positively to the inside, which is on the side of the leading leg.

Change of leg

To change the leading leg in the canter, the horse can do so through walk (simple change) and/or trot, or via a flying change.

Simple change

The horse carries out a transition directly to the walk and restarts into the canter with the other leg leading.

Aims

- To execute the movement smoothly.

- To remain on the bit.

- To maintain impulsion.

- To keep the hindquarters engaged.

- To remain straight.

The rider

The following example is for a simple change from left canter to right canter.

- Checks position.

- Ensures that the canter is collected enough.

- Gives the aids to walk.

- After the walk has been established, changes the aids from position left to position right and gives the aid to canter right.

The flying change of leg

This takes place during a period of suspension in the canter when both fore and hind legs should change together, the leading hind leg initiating the change.

Aims

- To remain light, calm and straight.

- To maintain impulsion.

- To maintain the same rhythm and balance.

- To achieve a noticeable and clean jump from one leading leg to the other (i.e. the change has expression).

The flying change should not be attempted before:

- The horse's hindquarters are strong.

- The horse has the ability to collect at the canter and to maintain impulsion.

- The horse is balanced and straight.

- The horse remains on the bit during his work.

- The canter strike-offs are correct.

Preparation

The horse should be asked to do simple changes at short intervals on alternate legs. When these are performed well, with a degree of collection, the horse remaining straight and 'on the aids', the trainer should ask for alternately true and counter-canter through the walk.

Execution

To make the first flying change as easy as possible for the horse, he is usually cantered across the school on a diagonal in a well-balanced, well-collected canter, and asked to change at the end of the diagonal. If the change has been made correctly, the horse should first be settled before being rewarded with a walk on a long rein. If the change was not correct or not made at all, the rider might try once more and, if again it is a failure, should then return to the preparatory exercises before retrying. It is essential that the change should not be late behind: i.e. the change is made first with the forelegs and then a stride or more later with the hind legs. Unless the rider can feel such an error from the saddle, an assistant on the ground should be employed to determine whether the change has been performed correctly.

Timing

In the case of a simple change through another gait this is not difficult, but to perform a flying change this must take place during the moment of suspension which follows the

1   2   3   4   5

Flying change of leg in canter. (1) The left canter starts with the thrust of the right hind, then the left foreleg leads (2). During the moment of suspension (4), the change takes place and the new lead begins, with the thrust of the left hind (5).

use of the horse's leading foreleg. Only then are all four feet off the ground and only then can the horse answer the aids and change the leading hind leg and hence the sequence.

The rider

For a flying change from left to right:

- Checks position.

- Makes a half-halt to improve the impulsion and balance and increase collection.

- Just before the leading leg comes to the ground, the rider changes the aids from position left to position right without collapsing the hips.

- Makes sure the horse's back muscles are allowed to swing.

It is important that the horse is kept straight and that the rider brings the new inside leg forward and the new outside leg back at the same moment. After the change the rider must keep the canter forward and active.

Alternative situations in which to ask for a change

Although many trainers teach their horses flying changes at the end of a diagonal, if the horse does not change correctly at the end of the diagonal, then other options can be tried. Some horses find the following positions easier. Also, when continuing the training it is essential to ensure that a horse does not anticipate and start to change of his own accord. Therefore, ask for the change from different positions.

- From the counter-canter, which can be executed down the long side of the school. To prevent anticipation the rider should sometimes continue in the counter-canter beyond the points at which the change is usually requested. It is most important for the horse to remain straight throughout the movement and to avoid any sideways drift. It is important, too, for the horse to change on the aids and not to anticipate.

- From the canter half-pass; allow one or two straight strides then ask for the change.

- In a serpentine ask for the change when crossing the centre line.

- From a 10m or 15m half-circle ask for the change when just about to return to the track.

Lateral work

Lateral work refers to any form of movement wherein at least one of the horse's hind feet moves in a different track from that of the forefeet. In lateral work the horse moves sideways as well as forwards. This helps to:

- Increase the obedience of the horse.

- Supple the horse, increasing the freedom of the shoulders, mobility of the hindquarters and the elasticity of that essential bond connecting the hindquarters, back, neck, poll and the mouth.

- To improve the cadence and balance.

- To help engage the hindquarters and so increase collection.

To achieve these objectives, the aims are:

- For gaits to remain free and regular.

- To maintain impulsion, rhythm and balance.

- To achieve a slight bend from the poll to the tail (except in leg yielding, when there is slight flexion only at the poll). The amount of bend depends on the suppleness and stage of training of the horse. It must never be so excessive (i.e. rider preoccupied with going sideways) that fluency, balance and impulsion are inhibited.

The turn on the forehand

The horse's hindquarters rotate around the forehand, away from the direction of the bend (see illustrations overleaf). This exercise is used to teach the rider the use of different leg and rein aids and to each the horse to move away from the leg.

The rider

- Corrects position.

- Maintains the walk or halts momentarily.

- Indicates the direction by asking for a slight bend to the inside and bringing weight slightly more on to the inside seat bone.

Turn on the forehand through 180º.

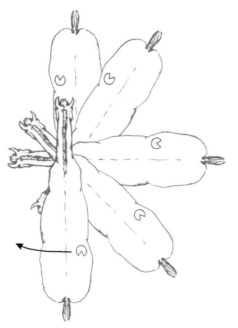

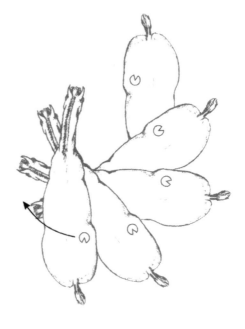

If the movement is carried out on the spot there is no engagement of the inside hind leg...

...it is better to walk around a small circle, since this will allow the inside hind leg to engage forward a little.

- Applies vibrant pressures with the inside leg on the girth, or, with a novice horse, very slightly back to encourage him to step sideways. Brings the outside leg slightly further behind the girth, where it can be applied to control the movement if the horse starts to move around too fast.

- Uses the outside rein to restrain the forward movement and to prevent the horse bending too much in the neck.

- Turns the body slightly in the direction of the bend. On completing the movement the horse is ridden forward by closing the outside leg and allowing with the hands.

Throughout the turn, coordination of the seat, legs and hands will make sure that the horse stays between the leg and hand and makes a supple turn, not evading forwards or backwards.

An alternative: The turn on the forehand ridden in the above manner results in the horse moving his hindquarters away from the direction of the bend. The turn on the forehand can also be executed by reversing the aids, when the rider's outside leg becomes the dominant one to cause the horse to step forward and in front of the inside hind leg as in travers (see page 177); the horse then moves the hindquarters in the direction of the bend.

Leg yielding

In the leg yield the horse moves forward and sideways. He should be straight, except for a slight flexion at the poll, allowing the rider to see the eyebrow and nostril on the inside. This bend is in the opposite direction from that in which he is moving. The inside legs pass and cross the outside legs. It is the easiest of the lateral movements, requiring no collection, and is therefore especially valuable in the training of young horses. It is used by many trainers as a means of introducing lateral work.

Execution

The first lessons are best given at the walk. Only when the horse understands the aids should it be tried at the trot. The usual figures for trying the leg yield are:

- From a 10m circle leg yield out to either the long side of the arena or to start a 20m circle.

- From the short side of the arena turn down the centre line and leg yield to the long side.

- Along the diagonal when the horse should be as close as possible parallel to the long side but with the forehand just in advance.

- Along the wall when the horse should not be at a greater angle than 35° to the direction in which he is moving.

As the most basic of the lateral movements, leg yielding can be carried out in walk and working trot. Hence, many riders and/or horses start lateral work with this exercise.

The rider

- Corrects position.

- Applies the inside leg by the girth. This is the dominant leg, causing the horse not only to step

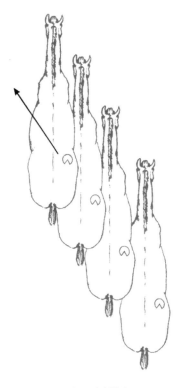

Leg yield left.

forward but also to bring his inside hind leg further under his body and slightly in front of the other hind leg.

- Keeps the outside leg just behind the girth and applies when necessary to keep the horse straight and to maintain the forward movement.

- Asks with the inside rein for a slight flexion at the poll so that the eye and arch of the horse's nostril can just be seen from the saddle.

- Uses the outside rein to regulate the flexion to help balance the horse and prevent the shoulder from falling out.

Shoulder-in

In shoulder-in, the horse, bent round the rider's inside leg and looking away from the direction of movement, travels forwards and sideways on three or four tracks. In the former (more commonly ridden form) the three tracks are formed as follows: 1) the inside forefoot; 2) the inside hind foot following the track of the outside forefoot; 3) the outside hind foot. In motion, the horse's inside foreleg passes and crosses in front of the outside leg; the inside hind leg is placed in front of the outside leg. The movement can be executed on straight lines or circles. It is most commonly performed in trot, and can be ridden in walk and canter to help straighten the horse.

Benefits

The shoulder-in is the foundation of all collected and advanced lateral work. Because of this, it is perhaps the most valuable of all exercises available to the trainer:

- It is a suppling and collecting movement, as the inside hind leg is brought well under the body and placed in front of the outside hind. To do this the horse must lower his inside hip and flex the joints of the hind leg.

- It helps the rider to control the shoulder of the horse. By 'thinking shoulder-in' when riding turns and circles, and particularly before striking

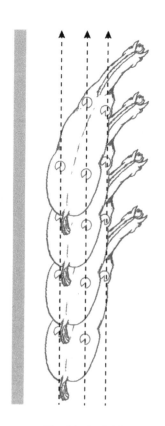

Shoulder-in right.

off to canter, it helps to prevent the shoulder falling out or the quarters coming in.

- It helps to make the horse straight.

- It improves the quality of the gaits.

- It can be used to discipline a horse.

Aims

- To maintain impulsion and willingness to go forward.

- To maintain rhythm.

- The bend should be through the body and not just the neck, otherwise the collecting value is lost and the shoulders tend to fall out.

- The hindquarters should not swing out (that is quarters-out instead of shoulder-in).

- The movement itself should go 'through' the horse: that is, the elastic bond between the hindquarters and mouth is maintained at all times.

Execution

Sometimes a first lesson is given at the walk, but as soon as the horse understands what is wanted, the movement should be executed at the trot. The usual way to begin the movement is on completion of a corner before the long side of the school. Instead of riding down the long side the rider continues on the curve of the corner, bringing the forehand away from the track but keeping the hind legs still on the track, where they should remain throughout the movement. The rider, when guiding the forehand off the track, increases the pressure from the inside leg and the

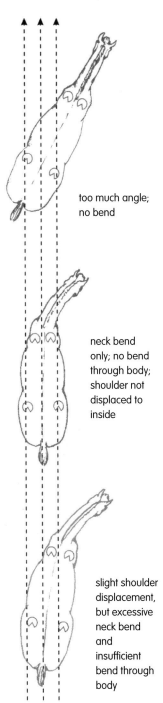

too much angle; no bend

neck bend only; no bend through body; shoulder not displaced to inside

slight shoulder displacement, but excessive neck bend and insufficient bend through body

Common faults in shoulder-in.

175

restraining action of the outside rein, while maintaining the bend with the inside rein and controlling the hindquarters with the outside leg.

At first, only a few steps of shoulder-in should be asked for, followed by the horse being ridden forward on a single track in the direction he is facing. The number of steps can be increased as performance and suppleness improve.

In shoulder-in the horse moves forwards and sideways on three or four tracks. He is bent around the rider's inside leg and moves away from the direction of the bend (see illustration on page 174). The horse must be able to show some engagement of the hind legs so that the gait is developing some collection.

The rider

- Checks position.

- Improves the impulsion and balance with a half-halt.

- Indicates the bend and direction with the inside rein.

- Increases the pressure of the inside leg on the girth to maintain the bend and further engage the horse's inside hind leg.

- Contains this extra impulsion by closing the fingers on the opposite (outside) rein, so preventing the horse from stepping straight forward and regulating the bend, particularly to prevent excessive neck bend.

- Rests the outside leg a little further behind the girth than the inside leg to support the bend and stop the hindquarters swinging out, just as on a circle.

- Turns slightly to the inside.

- Transfers slightly more weight to the inside.

- Keeps upright and in balance with the horse.

When the shoulder-in is ridden correctly, it should be possible to abandon the inside rein for a few steps without the horse losing his balance, impulsion, or rhythm.

If and when the rider's outside hand allows the horse to move straight forward again, he should do so immediately and return to a circle. However, in a dressage test the horse is usually brought back straight on the track or ridden into a movement such as medium trot.

The travers and renvers

In the travers (quarters-in) and the renvers (quarters-out) (shown on facing page), the horse is slightly bent around the inside leg of the rider and positioned at an angle of about 30° to the line of the track. They differ from the shoulder-in in that the horse looks in the direction in which he is moving. They can be performed along the wall or centre line. Primarily ridden in walk and trot, they can be used in canter too.

Benefits

- To increase obedience.

- To prepare for the half-pass.

- To increase the control over the hindquarters.

- As a collecting exercise in the canter they can be used in the preparation for the pirouette.

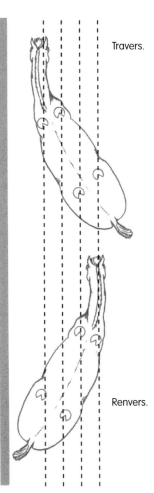

Travers.

Renvers.

Execution

The early lessons are usually given in the walk, but can later be carried out at trot and canter.

To execute travers: at the end of the short side, instead of straightening on to the track, the bend of the turn is maintained and the aids for travers are applied.

As the renvers is an inverted travers it uses the same muscles etc. as the travers.

The aids for travers and renvers are identical apart from the original positioning of the horse.

The rider

- Checks position.

- Improves the balance and impulsion with a half-halt.

- Asks for a bend with the inside rein and leg.

- Applies the outside leg behind the girth to move the hindquarters over.

- Controls the impulsion and the amount of bend with the outside rein.

The half-pass

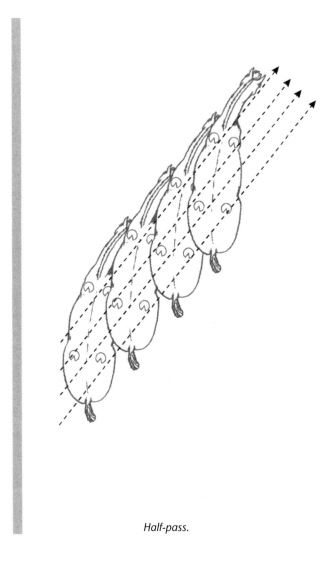

Half-pass.

This is a variation of travers, executed on the diagonal (see illustration above). The horse is slightly bent around the inside leg of the rider and should be aligned as nearly as possible parallel to the long side of the school, but with the forehand slightly in advance of the hindquarters. At trot and walk the outside legs cross and pass in front of the inside legs, but at the canter it is usual for the legs not to cross. The horse looks forward and sideways in the direction in which he is moving. The half-pass can be ridden at all three gaits.

Aims

- To maintain the same balance and rhythm throughout the entire movement.

- To maintain a bend, but this must not be so excessive that it leads to a loss of impulsion.

- To ensure the forehand is light so that there is freedom and mobility in the shoulders and ease and grace to the movement.

Execution

Correct execution depends greatly on how the horse goes into the movement and how well the forward element predominates. The trainer might begin the lesson with a half-volte followed by the half-pass. A useful alternative is shoulder-in along the short side and, as the corner is turned, half-pass across the diagonal; or to leg yield from the centre line to the long side and return to the centre line in half-pass.

The aids are similar to those for travers and renvers.

The rider

- Checks position.

- Improves the horse's balance and impulsion with a half-halt.

- Puts the horse into position right, or left, taking the forehand fractionally off the track.

- Looks and turns a little towards the point to which the movement is being made.

- Puts more weight into the inside stirrup.

- Keeps the forward movement and bend with the inside leg.

- Maintains the bend with the inside rein.

- Applies the outside leg behind the girth to encourage both the horse's outside legs to step forward and across the front of the two inside legs with rhythmical variations of pressure.

- Uses the outside rein to control the amount of forward movement and to prevent too much bend.

As the movement progresses, the outside leg aids are gradually increased so that the horse is finally straight (i.e. parallel) to the track or wall before being ridden forward on one track, or before changing to a half-pass on the other rein.

Half-pirouette at the walk

This is a half-circle performed on two tracks with a radius equal to the length of the horse. The forehand moves around the haunches. The forefeet and the outside hind foot move around the inside hind foot, which acts as the pivot, returning to the same spot or just in front of it each time it is lifted.

Aims

- The horse should be slightly bent to the direction in which he is moving.
- To remain on the bit.
- To maintain the rhythm of the walk.
- The horse should not move backwards.

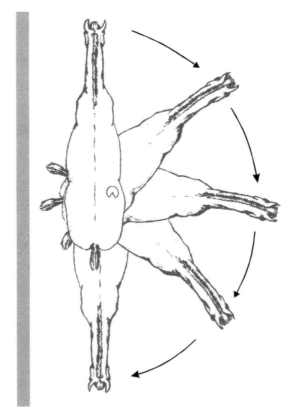

Half-pirouette.

Execution

The horse can be taught to respond to the aids for the walk pirouette by at first asking him for travers on a small circle. As he manages to retain the impulsion and sequence of the walk footfalls the size of the circle can be reduced until it becomes a walk pirouette.

Introducing the double bridle

The double bridle puts finishing touches, or the final polish, on movements which have already been taught and well executed when ridden in a snaffle. It can be worn after the horse has been introduced to lateral work and is accepting the bit in all work. Its first introduction should be with some simple work on a single track. Variations of stride length within a gait will help to establish good impulsion and will encourage the trainer to ride the horse on to the bit. The frequency of the use of the double bridle depends upon the rider and the horse.

Summary

When the horse is able to perform well all the school movements of the intermediate stage he should be a very good ride. It is a level of training which would benefit show jumpers; advanced event horses have to be able to do the work in order to perform the FEI Three-Day-Event Test.

More advanced training on the flat is not important for show jumpers or eventers, so the next chapter is usually treated as the sphere of the specialist dressage horse.

16. Advanced Training on the Flat

AT THIS STAGE THE RIDER/HORSE PARTNERSHIP BEGINS TO SPECIALISE. If dressage is chosen, ultimately: 'The dressage rider is an artist and the horse is his medium; together they produce a work of art' (Hans Handler). Only the great riders and horses can achieve this, but it should still be the aim of everybody embarking on this advanced training.

The more particular aims at this stage should be to train the horse to be:

- Responsive to delicate aids.

- Exceptionally supple in all gaits and movements.

- Able to generate great impulsion and collection.

To achieve these aims the rider must become:

- An analyst who pays great attention to detail and is quick to recognise faults and problems.

- Open-minded – ready to admit an error, eager to learn and, if necessary, willing to adjust the means of achieving the ends.

- Dedicated and able to work with enthusiasm day after day.

- Aware that no horse can perfect his movements unless he is skilfully ridden. The rider's balance, posture and correct application of aids become crucial and can only be developed and maintained through great determination and discipline.

Prerequisites and facilities

Facilities. At this stage, regular work is essential. It should be on good going, as hard, rough ground jars the horse and stiffens his back. It is also important to have enough

182

space to develop the extensions. Therefore, either a large indoor school or outdoor arena of 20m x 60m becomes a practical necessity.

Assistance. Help from a knowledgeable person on the ground is essential, not necessarily every day, but regularly, to check the rider's position and the horse's gaits and movements.

Horsemastership. Attention to detail includes the care of the horse, who needs:

- To be well fed as he must be very fit to do advanced work.

- Consistent grooming to keep him clean and to tone up his muscles.

- Constant attention to his physical well-being as strains, sores, etc., if not put right, will affect his work.

Objectives of training. The objectives remain the same as previously stated (see Chapters 11 and 12), though some should be nearer to achieving success than others. Thus, by this stage the horse should be submissive, straight, accepting the bit and secure in his rhythm in all three gaits. The major areas for improvement will be:

- Suppleness

- Impulsion

- Collection

General school work

With the possible exception of the turn on the forehand, all the exercises of the intermediate stage can be included in the basic school work.

The gaits

More time can be spent on the walk to develop the variations within this basic gait. The collected and extended walk must be developed, but with great care. An assistant on the ground should check that the sequence of footfalls remains true, for the rhythm is all too easily lost with so little impulsion being produced at the walk.

Greater variations within the trot and canter should be asked for, but taking care to develop enough impulsion to make this possible without hurrying in the extensions, or slowing down the tempo in the collections.

Circles

Ridden at the collected trot and canter these can be gradually reduced in size from 10m diameter to 6m diameter (a volte).

Aims

- The hindquarters should not swing inwards or outwards.
- To avoid excessive bend in the neck.
- Horse and rider should not lean in (or out).
- Rhythm is maintained during and when entering and leaving the circles.
- To perform circles equally well on both reins.

Serpentines

These should by now be relatively easy suppling exercises at the collected or working trot, and useful variations can be employed at the canter. Loops can be performed at the counter-canter as well as at the true canter, and the width of the loops can be reduced as the horse becomes more collected, so that the exercise becomes progressively more difficult: e.g. use a four-loop serpentine in a 20m x 60m arena at first and then progress to six loops. Flying changes can be executed on the centre line of the serpentine; however, simple changes are also a most useful suppling exercise and continually confirm submission and obedience.

Aims

- The loops to be of a similar size and shape.
- Simple or flying changes to be executed fluently and accurately.
- Rhythm to be maintained.
- Correct bend to be maintained.

Transitions

The following direct transitions can be practised:

Upward transitions:

- Halt to collected trot.

- Rein-back to collected trot or canter.

- Collected walk to collected canter.

- Halt to collected canter.

Later:

- Piaffe to collected trot.

- Piaffe to passage.

Downward transitions:

- Extension to collection at all three gaits.

- Collected walk, collected canter, and collected and medium trot to halt.

Later:

- Passage or piaffe to halt.

The **aims** of riding transitions are as previously stated (see pages 149–150).

Advancing the lateral work

The half-pass, travers and renvers should be executed with a greater degree of collection and sideways movement, but only insofar as the essential impulsion and fluency are maintained.

Counter change of hand (zigzag)

The counter change of hand (zigzag) is a series of half-passes either side of a line.

To execute at the trot

From a half-pass to the right the rider's outside (left) leg is used to direct the hindquarters slightly further over to the right and at the same time the horse's bend is changed so that the forehand can take the lead. The aids are then applied for a half-pass to the left. This will ensure that in the first steps of half-pass into the new bend on each occasion, the shoulders will be very slightly in advance of the quarters. Allowing the quarters to lead into a half-pass is a bad fault.

To execute at the canter

From a half-pass to the right the rider stops driving the horse laterally and rides him straight forward for two or three strides, during which time the change is asked for and the new bend to the left established before applying the aids for the half-pass left. When the horse can perform the change fluently and equally well from right to left half-pass or vice versa, the number of straight strides can be reduced ultimately to one, when the new bend is asked for during the change.

Aims

- The forehand must always lead in the half-pass.
- The horse must take strides of equal length in both directions of the half-pass, and should show the same degree of angle and bend on both reins.
- Impulsion, rhythm and balance must be maintained throughout the movement.

Advanced exercises

Flying changes in series

When the horse can execute single flying changes on the aids and in balance he should be ready to start a series of flying changes, which are executed regularly after a given number of strides. The number of strides between changes can be reduced as he masters the easier series from, say, five to two (two-time changes) and finally to changes every stride (one-time changes).

Execution

In these series the degree of collection should be slightly less than in the collected canter to ensure a good forward bound at each change.

One particular series should not be practised for too long, as the horse then tends to anticipate and will not change on the aids. The series and the number of changes asked in any series should be varied.

If teaching a more difficult series, end the lesson on one that is easy for him: that is, perform some four-time changes after doing some two- or one-time ones.

Aims

- Keeping the horse straight. Any tendency to drift or swing should be corrected by:

    1. Guiding the forehand, 'thinking shoulder-in', as each change is asked for.

    2. Increasing the impulsion, riding forward into the changes at a stronger canter: using the inside leg to achieve this.

- The change to be executed with the forelegs and hind legs changing simultaneously. If the change is late behind, this is usually a consequence of either the horse being on his forehand or the rider using too much rein and not enough leg. More impulsion and collection should be generated.

- Rhythm and impulsion must be maintained. If the horse moves more and more slowly through the series he should be ridden forward and asked to change at a medium canter. If he moves more and more quickly, half-halts should be applied during the strides when he is not changing.

Canter pirouette

The pirouette (half-pirouette) is a circle (half-circle) performed on two tracks, the circle having a radius equal to the length of the horse. The forehand moves around the hindquarters, the forefeet and the outside hind foot moving around the inside hind foot which is lifted and put down again on the same spot, or slightly in front of it.

Aims

- To keep the horse 'on the bit' with a light contact and a slight bend to the direction in which he is turning.

- To maintain balance, rhythm and impulsion.

- To maintain the regularity of the canter hoof beats. The inside hind leg is lifted and returned to the ground in the same rhythm as the outside hind foot, and should not remain on the ground.

- The strides should be accentuated, cadenced, and for a full pirouette should be six to eight in number and for a half-pirouette three to four.

The rider

- Collects the horse by a series of half-halts.

- Uses similar aids to those for half-pass, except the length of the stride is adjusted to reduce forward movement and produce a half-pass on the smallest circle.

Pirouettes and half-pirouettes may be ridden at the walk and later at the canter, but can only be achieved at the trot in piaffe.

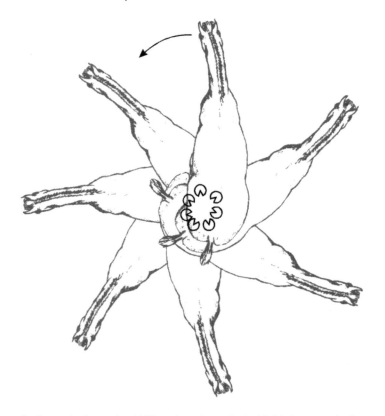

Pirouette: in theory the horse should lift and set down the inside hind on exactly the same spot, but in practice the inside hind leg makes a very small circle. The smaller this circle, the better the pirouette, provided that the rhythm of the gait is maintained.

Execution

The pirouette at the canter is one of the most difficult of all the advanced movements, as it calls for a high degree of collection and great impulsion. Horses should only be taught pirouettes after they have developed a good collected canter full of impulsion, are responding correctly to the half-halt, and are able to shorten the canter so much that for a few strides they almost remain on the spot (still in three-time) before willingly going forward again.

Various methods

- From a large walk pirouette and one in which the hindquarters are very well engaged, strike off into the canter while maintaining the same aids as for the walk pirouette. The horse should canter pirouette for a few steps before being cantered straight forward (if he lacks impulsion) or returning to the walk (if he becomes excitable). The success of this method depends on the strike-off being of high quality.

- From the renvers. At the end of a long side the rider asks for a very small half-circle (or passade) to canter in renvers parallel to the long side, and then turns towards the wall to perform a three-quarter pirouette. This method enables better control over the outside hind leg at the moment of starting the pirouette (one of the commonest faults is for the hindquarters to swing outwards). Also, the horse is already in the correct bend.

- From a large circle. This can be more difficult, as it is not so easy to prevent the hindquarters falling out, but is a useful progression after the above two methods. Voltes are performed within the large circle, eventually making them so small they become a passade and finally, a half-pirouette. Then proceed in counter-canter before trying on the other rein.

- From travers on a large circle, or from half-pass.

- From a straight line, but this should not be tried until the horse performs a satisfactory pirouette in the above methods. The rider should give the horse a slight shoulder-in position when approaching the point to which the pirouette is to be carried out, and the canter highly collected so that he is almost cantering on the spot when he is asked to turn into the pirouette.

If, during attempts at the pirouette, the horse moves into walk, it is important to keep asking with the aids for the pirouette, but with more vigour so that he returns to the canter. If he starts to swing around quickly, to swivel on his inside hind leg, return to work at the travers or renvers so that control over every collected stride can be maintained. Also, he can be asked to walk during the pirouette, perform a few steps of the pirouette at walk and then strike off into the canter, still in the pirouette, when more control over each stride should have been established.

It is essential during the pirouette for the rider to retain the correct position, to remain upright and fully seated in the saddle and to avoid tipping forward or to the outside with the momentum of the movement.

When working on pirouettes it is important to remember that they are demanding on the horse and should not be attempted for too long. It is important, too, for the size of the pirouette to be varied from half to three-quarter to whole, so that the horse remains on the aids and ready to come out of it whenever asked.

Piaffe

This is a highly collected, elevated and cadenced trot nearly on the spot.

Aims

- The height of the toe of the raised foreleg should be level with the middle of the cannon bone of the other foreleg; the forearm lifts towards the horizontal. The toe of the raised hind leg should reach just above the fetlock joint of the other hind leg.

Piaffe: maximum collection and engagement of the lowered hindquarters. There should be activity of the hind legs, lightness of the forehand, and proud submission.

- The neck should be raised and arched, the head perpendicular, the back supple and swinging, and the hindquarters slightly lowered, with active hocks well engaged to give great freedom, lightness and mobility to the shoulders and forehand.

- Each diagonal pair of legs should be raised and returned to the ground alternately with an even rhythm and a definite, but short, period of suspension.

- The piaffe should be produced as a result of great impulsion, so the horse should be ready and willing to move forward at all times.

- The horse should not move backwards, cross the forelegs, swing the forehand, or hindquarters, or take irregular steps.

- The horse should remain on the bit with a supple poll and a light rein contact.

The rider

- Corrects position.

- Uses both legs by the girth, either together or alternately, to ride forward into a restraining hand, but still with a light rein contact. The object is to ask the horse to bring both hind legs a little further under his body and so to lower his hindquarters and round his back.

- The rider sits lightly to allow the horse to round and move 'through' his back, but in an erect position, with the seat bones forward to encourage forward impulsion.

- As the horse comes into piaffe, the rider indicates the rhythm by increasing and decreasing leg pressure without removing them from the horse's sides. Once the horse has understood, the rider must be careful to take up the rhythm offered by the horse.

A well-trained horse in correct equilibrium will only require a light but consistent contact with the rein to hold him in piaffe, and should always be ready to move straight forward into passage or another gait.

At an intermediate standard, the horse should be allowed to gain a little ground, but advanced horses should stay on one spot for ten to twelve steps.

Execution

The piaffe can be taught either from the ground or from the saddle. In the former method it is easier for the horse to use his back without the weight of the rider, but some horses find the latter easier to understand.

Teaching from the ground

These lessons should take place in an enclosed arena and the stages are as follows:

1. The horse is brought to the middle of the arena, fitted with a snaffle, saddle, cavesson, lunge rein and side-reins. The side-reins should be adjusted so that they just make contact when the horse is collected. It may be necessary to shorten them as he becomes more collected. The lunge rein is attached to the cavesson and the horse is taken to the track on the left rein, as this is the easier for most horses and convenient for the trainer.

2. The trainer, positioned near the shoulder of the horse, takes up a fairly short rein in the left hand and, holding the whip in the right hand, walks the horse slowly once or twice around the arena. As soon as the horse is walking in a calm and relaxed manner, he can be asked to trot. The hind legs should initiate this transition and the steps should be short. If the horse tries to go forward too much, the trainer should apply restraining aids with the hand. If the horse is reluctant to go forward, he should be touched with the whip just above the hind fetlocks. The voice should be used to supplement these driving and restraining aids. When the horse can work calmly and with rhythm in this exercise, the teaching of piaffe can begin.

3. With the horse standing correctly at halt on a long side of the arena, the trainer should be positioned, as before, alongside the horse's shoulder with the whip in the right hand. The trainer will now take up a very short rein, holding the left hand closely behind the horse's head (see opposite). From the halt the horse should be asked to move forward with a few steps of very collected trot and then brought again to the halt; this time the trainer should move to stand directly in front of the horse. The horse will soon come to understand that the trainer at his side means activity, and that the trainer in front means immobility.

   Eventually the aim must be for the horse to work on both reins, but for the first day the trainer may be satisfied with a few good steps on one rein. Over a series of lessons the trainer should progressively ask the horse to shorten the trot strides and should increase the collection. The hind legs must come further under the body; to encourage them to do so and to spring elastically off the ground, the trainer can use the whip to touch the hind legs. Only a few strides at a time should be asked for in this manner.

4. When seven or eight perfectly level steps can be executed without moving forward further than 0.9m (1 yard), the horse may be ridden: but the rein should still be in the hands of the trainer, who continues to control the horse from the ground in the same manner as before. Eventually, the trainer can ride the horse to perfect the movement.

The trainer's main considerations should be:

- Never to ask too much. The horse has to work hard to produce the necessary impulsion and bouncy spring to his action, so the lessons should not last too long and should end if possible, on a good, calm note.

- The horse must remain straight. If he tries to bring his hindquarters in from the wall, the trainer should counter with a slight shoulder-in position.

- The strides must be level. The trainer should never sacrifice levelness through efforts to produce more elevated steps.

- The horse should always move forward – if only 2.5cm (1in) per step – until training has reached its final stage, when ten to twelve steps on the spot will be the aim.

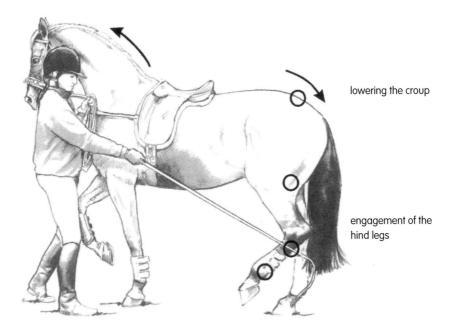

lowering the croup

engagement of the hind legs

Training piaffe from the ground.

- The hind legs should not be brought too far under the body or the hindquarters will be over-burdened. The horse will then have difficulty in lifting his hind feet off the ground, which tends to make the trot irregular and the forward transitions abrupt.

Teaching from the saddle

This method, although usually easier for the trainer (since it should offer more control), makes it more difficult for the horse to use his back elastically.

The principal considerations and progressive training methods are similar to those outlined in training from the ground. An assistant trainer walks alongside the horse's hindquarters. The rider applies the aids for piaffe, and the assistant, if necessary, taps with the whip to encourage the horse to flex his hind legs and to place them further under his body. As soon as the horse steps correctly with diagonal pairs, the forelegs rising higher than the hind legs, he can be asked to carry out this work more energetically. To achieve this the collection has to be built up so that just before asking for piaffe-like steps, walk pirouettes and transitions from a shortened trot to halt (and vice versa) can be performed.

It is advisable to teach piaffe first, but if the horse is naturally short of impulsion, the passage may be taught before the piaffe, not only to improve the impulsion but to teach the horse to spring energetically off the ground.

Passage

This is a very collected, very elevated and very cadenced trot. Each diagonal pair of feet is raised higher and with a longer period of suspension than for any other trot.

Aims

- The toe of the raised foreleg should be level with the middle of the cannon bone of the other foreleg. The toe of the raised hind leg should be slightly above the fetlock joint of the other hind leg, i.e. as in piaffe.

- The neck should be raised and arched, with the poll as the highest point and the head close to the perpendicular. The horse should remain on the bit, accepting a light contact.

- The hindquarters should be well engaged and the flexion of the knees and hocks should be accentuated, but with graceful elasticity of movement.

- The impulsion should be lively and pronounced and the horse should be able to go smoothly from the passage to the piaffe, and vice versa, without apparent effort and without altering the rhythm.

- The steps should be regular and neither the forehand nor the hindquarters should swing from one side to the other.

Execution

The passage is taught usually from the saddle. It is developed out of the piaffe, the collected trot, or sometimes the walk, depending on the abilities and temperament of the horse. It is most usual to teach it from the piaffe, as long as the horse has mastered this movement.

The horse is ready to be taught passage when he is capable of positive collection and extension, and of containing his impulsion.

It may be useful to have an assistant on the ground, who can come close to the hindquarters, with a long whip if necessary, and without upsetting the horse can indicate that more impulsion and elevation are required.

The rider applies the leg aids, the pressures being in the rhythm of the passage, and sits deep, using the forward-driving influence of the seat (page 91). The hands restrain, saying 'no faster', so that the increased impulsion goes upwards to produce passage – the elevated steps gaining little ground. When passage-like steps are achieved they should be maintained just long enough for the horse to understand that this is what is required and then he should be given a reward.

Passage: maximum collection and engagement, with the horse moving forward in a very cadenced, elevated trot.

The rider can **reduce** the leg pressure when the horse goes into passage and cease the pressure when requiring the horse to return to trot.

As with piaffe, regularity in all its aspects is of prime importance. Only when this can be achieved and maintained should the trainer strive for greater elevation. The movement should be smooth and flowing, without jerky prop-like landings of the forelegs, or hollowing of the back.

Care must be taken that the long whip, used to stimulate activity by applying it to the hindquarters, is not employed too much or too often, so that its stimulating effect is lost.

Variations of passage

Each horse has his characteristic natural type of trot, which should appear in his piaffe and passage. This is why there is so much variation in the types of passage performed. Ideally, the speed of the rhythm (tempo) remains the same in piaffe and passage.

Dressage competitions

Many serious riders aim to compete in dressage competitions and to achieve success the following are important prerequisites:

- To have a relaxed horse at the competition. This usually entails frequent visits to shows, whether competing or not, especially with high-spirited, temperamental or young horses.

- Careful organisation of the 'riding-in' period, taking into account the character and abilities of the horse and the test to be performed. The work to be included (lungeing, walking around, loosening up, etc.) and the time it will take should be planned beforehand.

- Study of judges' sheets to ascertain the defects which need most attention and then training accordingly.

- Development of 'arena craft' which entails careful study of the test to be performed, accurate execution of it, good use of the arena, and determination to show off the horse at his best.

17. Training the Horse to Jump

HORSES ARE BORN WITH VARYING DEGREES OF JUMPING ABILITY. The trainer's task is to develop the horse's ability, giving him the confidence to jump many different types of obstacles and to do so when carrying a rider.

The horse's jumping technique

A horse jumping correctly from a balanced, calm, yet energetic approach to an obstacle appears to do so with ease. During the last few strides of the approach he stretches his head and neck forward and downwards, then raises them to spring upwards off his forehand. This takes place a moment before the hind feet meet the ground. The powerful muscles of the hindquarters and thighs, and the leverage of the hips, stifles, hocks and fetlocks, push the horse upwards and forwards over the obstacle.

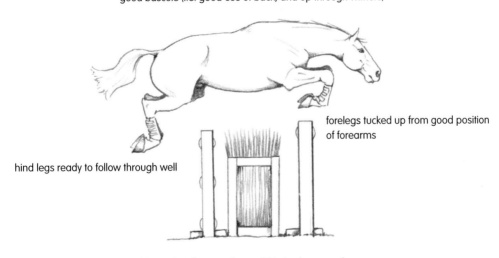

good bascule (i.e. good use of back, and up through withers)

forelegs tucked up from good position of forearms

hind legs ready to follow through well

Horse showing good use of his body over a fence.

During take-off and over the obstacle, the horse's back should be rounded, not hollow, with the withers as the highest point and with the head and neck stretched forward to help his balance (known as basculing).

On descent, the head and neck rise slightly and the forelegs meet the ground one after the other, followed by the hind legs.

This style is the most efficient method of jumping and demands least effort from the horse. But it takes time to build up the muscles and to develop the suppleness to enable him to jump in this way. Rushed training usually results in incorrect muscle development, less efficient styles (e.g. a hollow back in mid-air) and often eventually – because it takes an effort to jump – a loss of confidence and refusal.

The muscles which should be developed through flatwork, riding out, especially up and down hills, and gymnastic jumping exercises, are as follows:

- The upper neck muscles, not those on the underside.

- The shoulder and forearm.

- Back and loin, which are probably the most important.

- Second thigh muscles.

The training programme

The work for at least the first year of the horse's ridden life is common to an eventer, a show jumper and a dressage horse. He should be backed as described in Chapter 9, and trained on in the way described in Chapter 13.

Flatwork is essential in order to develop the correct muscles and the controlled riding necessary to jump in the above style. In the case of the potential show jumper, greater emphasis can be placed on jumping in conjunction with this flatwork. Easy obstacles should be used so that he gradually builds up his ability and confidence.

When he is being backed, and during the early riding days, he can be lunged over trotting poles and very small fences. If the facilities are available he could be loose-schooled. After he relaxes when ridden, and when he is sufficiently obedient and fit, the rider can take him over trotting poles, then progress gradually to small obstacles, with the size and variety of the fences being slowly increased.

The rate of progress will depend upon the ability of the horse and rider, but the essential factors are:

- The jumping should be fun for the horse, so he must not be asked too much for his stage of training, nor should he be asked to jump when tired. Schooling sessions over fences should be short.

- Slightly more difficult fences may be tackled when the horse can jump the easier obstacles in the styles described above, but if at any time he loses his confidence, return to the easier obstacles. It is important that in each jumping lesson he is loosened up over trotting poles and/or small fences; gradually progressing to larger obstacles.

Lungeing over small obstacles

The horse first learns to jump without a rider on his back, on the lunge. Start by walking over a pole on the ground, progress to trotting over a series of poles and to jumping solid single obstacles. Remember at all times that it is difficult for the horse to jump off a turn and it takes great skill and experience on the part of the lunger to give him the necessary assistance. Therefore, for most trainers it is advisable to restrict the work on the lunge to trotting poles and single obstacles of not more than about 1m (3ft 3in). For techniques of lungeing over obstacles see pages 135–136.

Loose-schooling over obstacles

If the horse can be encouraged to jump loose, calmly, rhythmically and with impulsion, he will learn to look after himself and to develop a good style of jumping. Damage can be done with inadequate facilities, and/or inexperienced trainers, resulting in the horse running out, refusing, or starting to rush his fences. Like lungeing, loose-schooling is only of value if done well.

Requirements

- An indoor school or small enclosure from which it is impossible for the horse to escape, or a jumping lane consisting of a series of small fences.
- If an indoor school or enclosure is used, the obstacles should have wings to discourage the horse from running out.
- The horse should be obedient to aids of the voice and the lunge whip.

Technique

The horse, wearing a headcollar or cavesson and protective boots, should be led around the school once or twice and then let loose and sent round at the trot, driven on when necessary by his trainer's voice and lunge whip. An assistant is needed and should be responsible for driving the horse forward in one half of the school. The trainer and assistant should never be in front of the horse as he moves round the track.

When the horse trots calmly and willingly around the school, an obstacle with wings can be erected. It is advisable to place the poles on the ground, and only when the horse trots over them confidently should they be raised. The best position for the obstacle is usually soon after the corner. Placing poles (see page 202), of 2.4–2.75m (8–9ft), or 5.5–6.1m (18–20ft) in front of the fences are advisable to stop the horse rushing, or arriving at an awkward take-off position. Alternatively, a pole can be placed diagonally in the corner and the small obstacle 16m (52ft) away from it.

It is essential for the trainer and the assistant to present the horse straight at the fence and not to chase him into it. It is also essential for the horse to jump of his own accord, encouraged by the voice and the presence of the whip. Obstacles should never be 'trappy', nor too high. At a later stage multiple fences may be used.

The horse should be rewarded frequently during loose-schooling sessions. After a few good circuits he should be stopped, patted, and occasionally given titbits.

Jumping with a rider

The horse should be ready to jump with a rider only after he has learned to jump without a rider, has been backed, is fit and responsive to the aids.

General principles

- It is advisable when jumping to have an assistant present to put up obstacles, to ensure that the distances between fences are correct, and also for reasons of safety.

- The obstacles should be solid or substantial so that the horse does not become careless through finding it easy to hit fences. At the same time, they should be 'inviting', to encourage him to jump and not to run out, and should be kept small enough to prevent him being overfaced.

- Distances between the obstacles and the placing and trotting poles should be 'correct' until an advanced stage of training.

- The young horse should be started over fences with which he is familiar and which he has jumped successfully on the lunge. When trying a 'strange' obstacle it is advisable to make it small in height; to show it to him first; to let him sniff at it; and with nervous horses, to follow an experienced horse over the fence. At all costs, refusals should be avoided.

- Jumping can cause strain on a young horse's tendons and feet. Sprains and lameness can result, particularly if the ground is too hard or too soft, or if the horse is not fit enough for the work demanded. Long jumping sessions should be avoided.

NB There is no need to jump massive fences at home. The aim of the trainer is to familiarise the horse with all types of obstacles and to develop a style which will make jumping as easy as possible. This can be achieved over low obstacles, and even advanced horses need not practise over more than 1.2m (4ft) obstacles.

Method of riding

In order to do this work without hindering the horse, the rider must be competent and confident. Although remaining in control the rider should not try to 'place' the horse (adjusting his stride so that he takes off in a particular position). After presenting the horse straight at the obstacle, the rider should have the following aims in mind:

- To sit as still as possible in the correct position.

- To retain a light rein contact.

- Although allowing the horse as far as possible to approach and jump the obstacles in his own way, sufficient impulsion is essential and at times the rider might have to generate this through use of the legs and – if necessary – with the seat and taps of the whip.

- The horse will find it easier to jump in the correct style if he approaches the fence in balance, and therefore with rhythm. Thus the rider should help the horse to establish a rhythm and should not rush or shorten up into a fence.

In the early stages of jump training, the horse should be fitted with a neck strap or a breast plate – which on occasion even the most experienced rider may need to hold (or the mane) in order to avoid interfering with the horse's mouth.

The correct position for the rider is described in Chapter 2. It is usual with a young horse to adopt the forward seat, out of the saddle, in order to give the horse's back the freedom to work. However, the seat aids can be used momentarily with a horse who tries to stop, or who lacks impulsion. When working over trotting poles it is essential for the horse's back to be able to move freely and not to be made rigid or hollow. It is usual, therefore, to adopt rising trot; although sitting trot in a forward seat is acceptable for a rider with a good seat and a horse who is strong and supple in his back.

The stages of training

Trotting poles

Work over poles on the ground, at first singly and then in series, is an essential part of a young horse's general education. It is a useful gymnastic exercise which teaches him to lower his head and neck, to round his back, to flex his joints and also to coordinate the action of his limbs.

Distances between poles

Whether on the ground or raised, these must accommodate the horse's stride exactly. For most horses and ponies, except very small ones, the optimum distances are 1m (3ft 3in) for the walking and 1.3–1.35m (4ft 3in–4ft 6in) for trotting. The latter is based on the trotting stride of the average horse. Uncoordinated or big horses need 1.5m (5ft); ponies may need 1.2m (4ft). It is essential to maintain correct distances between poles on the ground. Slight adjustments should be made to suit the strides of different horses and the going (for example heavy going needs shorter distances). An assistant on the ground should be ready to re-position displaced poles or to adjust distances when they do not suit the stride of the horse.

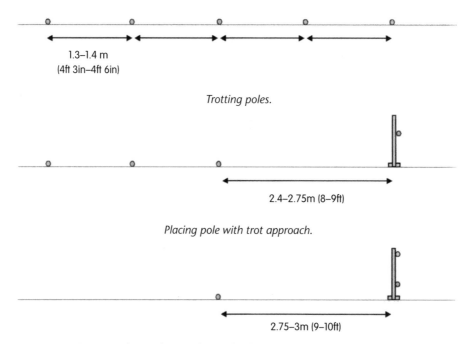

1.3–1.4 m
(4ft 3in–4ft 6in)

Trotting poles.

2.4–2.75m (8–9ft)

Placing pole with trot approach.

2.75–3m (9–10ft)

A canter pole to a fence to be used with an experienced horse and rider.

If poles are to be raised they are best put on blocks which have been slightly hollowed out to enable the pole to be fitted and not to roll when hit. Light plastic blocks are ideal.

Technique

First walk the horse over a single pole. When he does this calmly, the number can be increased to two, three and then four. The poles can then be altered to trotting distances. It is important for the horse to remain calm and to maintain a rhythm. If he gets excited, it sometimes helps to remove alternate poles. He can be trotted in a circle until he settles, and when he does so the poles can be tried again.

Introducing obstacles

When the horse trots over the poles correctly and calmly, a very small obstacle can be erected beyond the last trotting pole. It should look inviting, should not exceed 38cm (1ft 3in) in height, and preferably should consist of cross poles which direct the horse towards the centre of the fence. The aim is for the horse to land over the last pole and, without taking a stride, take off over the obstacle. The average horse needs between 2.4m (8ft) and 2.75m (9ft) in front of the fence. Distances should be adjusted for long- or short-striding horses.

Placing poles

In order to help the horse arrive at a good position for take-off, especially in the early stages, when the rider should not interfere, it is advisable to use either trotting poles as above, or a single placing pole, which should be 2.4–2.75m (8–9ft) in front of the fence.

Types of obstacle

As soon as the horse can jump a particular fence at the end of a line of trotting poles, or after a placing pole, calmly and in good style, he can be asked to jump a slightly higher, wider, or different type of obstacle in the same manner.

Single fences

The horse must gradually be introduced to fences (which have ground lines) without trotting poles or a placing pole. The horse should learn to think for himself and should adjust his stride. If a horse starts to rush the fence with inexperienced riders (and for the first few jumps in any lesson) reversion to use of a placing pole is of value.

Combinations

The horse must gradually be introduced to series of fences between which he can take one or two strides. These should start very low so that the horse can gain his confidence.

A placing pole is usually introduced at the beginning of a series of fences to help the horse meet the first one correctly.

A placing pole is usually advisable in front of a small upright, then another fence at one stride (5.5m/18ft) to a second fence at two strides (8.2m/27ft).

As the horse becomes more confident and proficient, extra fences can be added and the heights and distances altered. The aim is to have the horse jumping in good style with a clear take-off platform.

This means:

- His forelegs and hind legs should take off from almost the same place.

- He should bend his forelegs upwards, not backward, and they should remain a pair.

- He should jump straight and not twist in the air.

- He should jump calmly and in a good rhythm.

The distances between fences which suit most horses are in multiples of 2.75m (9ft) to 3.35m (11ft) with the fences not over 1m (3ft 3in). If the horse bends his forelegs backwards, the distances are too short; if he flattens in outline between the fences, the distances are too long. The first fence should always be the smallest with the last fence the largest.

By altering the distances the horse can be taught to shorten and lengthen his stride and thus become more athletic. It is important to alter both heights and distances very gradually so that he does not lose confidence.

Cantering

The non-jumping strides at the above distances are taken at the canter, but the initial approach should be at the trot. In the early stages of jump training it is advisable to approach all the fences at the trot as at this gait the horse is usually more balanced and the slower speed encourages him to bascule. However, some trainers work exclusively in canter from the start of a horse's training. Some riders allow their horses to break into canter just before the obstacle, but it is not advisable to make the entire approach at canter until the horse's work on the flat at this gait is satisfactory, and the fences are higher than about 1m (3ft 3in). At the canter the horse takes tiny obstacles in his stride naturally, but this does not develop his bascule and will encourage a rather flat jump.

Changing the distances

When the horse jumps combinations and grids with correct distances, calmly and in a fluent style, then the distances can be varied, but by inches only at a time, to teach him to jump from both long and short strides. It is best to keep any series of fences either for short strides or for long. Altering short and long distances is very difficult and is inadvisable for all except top horses and riders.

Varying the fences

The horse must be taught to jump all types of fences with confidence. He should be introduced to miniature versions of all the fences found in the show ring – brightly coloured obstacles, walls, triple bars, oxers, planks, brushes, barrels, etc. When riding out, every opportunity can be taken to jump the young horse over unfamiliar obstacles, such as ditches, banks, hedges, logs, etc., as long as they are low enough not to overface the pupil.

Tackling water jumps should also come into the training programme. Firstly, the horse must learn not to be frightened of water, so he can be walked through puddles and made to jump small streams and ditches, preferably following a more experienced horse. He must have encountered a water tray under a fence and learnt to jump with confidence. A water tray can vary in width from 0.9m (3ft) to much wider and is a common sight in many show jumping classes. The first water jump he is asked to attempt should not be wide (a maximum of 1.2m/4ft). It is also advisable to put a pole of about 0.9m (3ft) high over the centre of the water to encourage him to jump into the air, not just to pop over the brush into the water.

The rider should try to get the horse to approach the water with a little more speed than for a normal fence and to ask him to take off as close as possible to the water.

Courses

A horse who is to compete must learn to jump series of fences other than in straight lines. Therefore, a short course of fences similar to, but fewer in number and smaller in height than those in the show ring can be erected. The rider should try to give the horse the best possible approach to the fence:

1. Corners must not cut; the horse should be given as many straight strides before the fence as possible.

2. The horse must be kept balanced and in a rhythm. To do this the rider will probably need to half-halt and collect the horse immediately on landing over each fence and to make a great effort to turn each corner correctly.

3. The horse must have enough impulsion to tackle the fences, but impulsion must

not be confused with speed. Going fast will tend to make the horse flatten over the fences.

Jumping at speed

Most jump-offs are against the clock, so any horse and rider having had sufficient training to make winning a possibility must learn how to jump a course at speed. Galloping into the fences is rarely advisable with young horses, who tend to flatten and become careless. The horse must learn to jump fences at angles and to be balanced enough to cut a corner and – having taken one or two strides – to jump the obstacle.

The rider should aim to maintain impulsion and rhythm when practising these techniques over small obstacles.

Solving jumping problems

Refusing

This is a problem which the trainer should try to avoid at all costs. Therefore never ask a horse to jump a fence at a height which he and his rider are not capable of negotiating. With strange obstacles, give the horse every opportunity to gain his confidence by starting very low, by having a more experienced horse jump first, and by making the fence as inviting as possible with a ground line, good width and wings to stop run-outs.

Should the horse refuse, if it is through lack of confidence or poor riding, lower the fence before trying again. If the horse is doing it out of mischief and is starting to do it frequently, he should be reprimanded once, and ridden strongly into fences.

If a horse who normally jumps well starts refusing, it is probable that he is in pain. Steps must be taken to discover the reason. It may be his feet, his back or his mouth that is hurting him.

Rushing

Rushing into a fence makes it difficult for the horse to be balanced and to arrive at the correct take-off position. It is often considered to be a result of over-eagerness: but, on the contrary, it is usually caused by lack of confidence and the horse trying to get the frightening operation (of jumping) over as quickly as possible.

To correct

- The rider must give the horse confidence, which is best done by jumping frequently over small single fences, so that it becomes part of the routine rather than a major operation. Consecutive fences should not be attempted. After jumping one fence, the horse should be settled before attempting another.

- The rider can circle the horse in front of the fence until he settles into a rhythm, and only then allow him to jump.

- Trotting poles can be placed in front of the obstacle. It is usually best to walk into the first pole of the line.

- Small grids can be used frequently.

- Jump on a circle with a short approach.

Rushing after the fence. It is important for the horse to be balanced as soon as possible after the fence and not to rush off. If the voice and half-halts (but not pulling on the reins) are not effective then place a pole at either 6.4m (21ft) or 9.4m (31ft) after the fence.

Taking off too close

Horses who take off too close to a fence lack scope and/or confidence.

To correct

- The horse must be given sufficient impulsion to clear the fence.

- A take-off rail should be placed about a 30cm (1ft) out from the base of each fence.

- The distances between combination fences can be gradually lengthened so that he learns to extend his stride and to take off further away.

- Use placing poles to get the horse to stand back.

Jumping with a hollow back

Horses tend to jump with a flat or hollow back if they approach the fences too fast and/or take off far away.

To correct

- Jump fences out of a trot rather than a canter.

- Use placing poles in front of the fences to encourage him to get closer to the fences. Begin with a distance which is easy for him, and gradually shorten it so that he has to take off closer to the fence.

- Jump plenty of low, wide parallels which encourage a horse to bascule and to fold his forelegs.

- Use plenty of grids with relatively short distances between the fences.

Familiarisation

A horse's first show is usually a nerve-racking experience. It is therefore advisable to take him to a show before he starts competing and to get him relaxed in this stimulating atmosphere.

18. Cross-country Riding

ALTHOUGH THE THREE PHASES OF EVENTING ARE OF EQUAL IMPORTANCE, the cross-country is often the main reason for riders to participate in the sport and is often the most dominant phase.

The rider and horse need a high level of skill in all three phases, but the most challenging within eventing is to link up the three phases so that the work complements and improves, rather than spoils, each phase, i.e. what is done in dressage must not hinder the cross-country, or what is done in the cross-country must not hinder the show jumping. It is a high level of horsemanship, and understanding of the horse's basic training, that will achieve a high standard in each of the three disciplines, not separately, but together, which defines the skills of an event rider.

In this chapter we are going to concentrate on the actual cross-country phase, but you will see and hopefully understand the links to the other two phases.

Cross-country riding will test the rider's balance, judgement, courage, agility, and quickness of reaction and the horse's courage, agility and obedience.

There are two aspects to being effective and competitive in the cross-country phase – the jumping of the fences and the riding – in particular the ability to maintain a gallop between them.

Galloping and the galloping seat

Often at events one sees riders going cross-country, especially at Novice or Junior level, with horses pulling hard – sometimes out of control – or riders who are trying to get lazy or slow horses to go faster bumping up and down on their backs, as a consequence of poor technique. One is aware that this sort of riding could lead to problems later on when upgrading to Intermediate or Advanced or doing a CCI.

It is obvious that a horse galloping in balance on a line in good rhythm is going to take less out of himself, run less risk of injury, be able to jump better and more economically and therefore save time. Also it will give him an outlet for built-in inhibitions and tension which, together with the development of his natural balance and rhythm, will be of great benefit in the dressage work.

To achieve the above it is important that the horse is galloping true and using himself in the right way, and that the horse and rider feel comfortable together when galloping. This can be achieved by taking a leaf out of the race riders' book and, whilst galloping in training and doing fittening work, adopting a touch of the jockey's position. We are not looking for the jockey's position in a finish, but more the sort of position a jockey would have while cantering a horse down to the start of a race – maintaining the horse's stride well below racing pace, with the rider's leg at the girth (under no circumstances behind it), the seat well out of the saddle, the rider's back straight and with length, and the line between the horse's mouth and the rider's elbow straight, in other words the elbow to the hand is an extension of the rein.

Controlling the horse while galloping requires a rapport with the horse through the reins. The rider's hold on them is not too strong nor too light; the horse should like it, feel it, and respond to it. It is like feeling a fish on the line when fishing. The rider must create a sense of balance – while balancing the horse the rider balances *on* the horse at the same time. The horse is not constantly being pushed with seat or leg, but encouraged to draw into the contact as described above. It is right when the rider will feel as if the horse can go on forever.

As the cross-country is as influential as the dressage and show jumping it should be practised to the same extent. By starting to practise this at slow speed and gradually building up the speed the rider should also develop a sense of what is the correct cross-country speed.

Cross-country jumping

As described in the previous section, between fences the rider should usually be out of the saddle in the galloping seat. On approaching the fence, the rider should be able to come with the seat closer to the saddle, sometimes even sitting down in the saddle. The rider should be looking at the fence as a whole, and then, on nearing the fence, looking beyond it. Where there are combinations and lines of fences related to each other the rider should look at the next element. This will assist in choosing and staying on the correct line. The lower leg should be at the girth, with the stirrup leather hanging straight down and the stirrup on the widest part of the foot. The rider should be positioned in the middle of the horse and *never in front of the horse's movement.* On the approach to the fence riders should imagine having two-thirds of the horse in front of them. The hand must be soft enough to allow the horse to position his head where he can study and focus on the fence. In some situations the rider would need to allow the rein to slip through the hand without losing the contact. On the landing side of the fence, particularly where there is a drop, the rider's lower leg should come forward and the upper body should come up and back and the reins should slip through the hands to allow the horse to balance himself on landing. After the fence the rider should go with the horse and move the horse forward.

On the cross-country course the horse and rider will meet a lot of different types of fences, but in principle these can be divided into five different categories. When walking the course the rider must study and decide in which gait, speed, rhythm and line to approach the fence, i.e. the rider needs to be in the correct 'gear' with the engine revving at the correct 'revs' and, like a motor racing driver, be on the correct racing line.

The five categories of cross-country fences are:

1. Sloping fences with good ground line e.g. steeplechase fence, ascending spread – these types of fences can be jumped out of the horse's galloping stride and rhythm and should not require too much setting up or gear change.

2. Single fences with upright front e.g. oxers, gates – these fences require a certain amount of precision so therefore rider needs to set up and approach at a steadier more controlled canter.

3. Steps up and flat ascending spreads e.g. triple bars – the rider needs to be able to change down in gear, produce a rounder, bouncier stride and then, on that stride, without lengthening it, slightly accelerate to the fence.

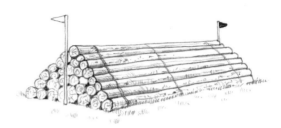

Log pile – a useful obstacle which can be jumped from either direction.

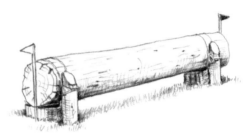

Hanging log.

Bench, or seat, fence.

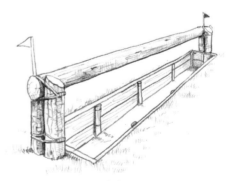

Trakehner.

A rails–ditch–rails complex. The rails should be fixed, so that if hit by a horse he does not carry them down the bank with him, which could cause a fall.

4. Problem fences e.g. bounces, drops, combinations, water – rider needs to change down in gears to go slow enough for the horse to see what is there, figure out what to do and then do it, but still create enough forward impulsion so that the horse will take on the fence. 'Third gear', short, bouncy stride into hand into fence.

5. Narrow and precision fences – 'skinnies' – these fences are often placed in relation to other fences, in combinations, related distances or doglegs. The rider needs to put the horse in the right gear i.e. speed, that enables the horse to maintain the correct line, and allows the horse to understand that he needs to go between the flags. On the approach the rider needs to keep the horse between leg and hand to maintain the horse's line and focus.

There are variations of fences within the above categories, and riders could possibly come across fences that would fall outside these categories; therefore they have to be prepared to vary their technique but still use the basics of approaching the fence in what is the correct gear and line for that fence.

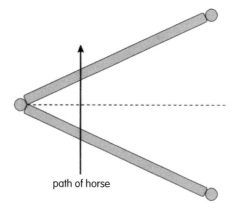

path of horse

A corner fence showing the safest path for the horse: i.e. at right angles to a line which bisects the corner.

Schooling and preparation

It should be recognised that the schooling for cross-country, and the work to get the horse fit to cope with the speed and endurance elements of the cross-country phase, are equally as important as the preparation for dressage and show jumping. Any cross-country schooling and fitness work should always be done on the best possible ground, and it is advisable to avoid firm ground as this could lead to an increased risk of injury to the horse. Very wet or slippery ground can dent the horse's confidence if he does not feel secure when turning or at the take-offs and landings of fences.

The purpose of schooling cross-country is to build confidence in the horse and teach him about different types of fences so that he develops his skill to cope. He particularly needs to build confidence in the jumping of ditches and water jumps as these fences present a factor of the unknown to the horse, as do some drop fences and those where the lines might not be immediately clear to the horse.

Schooling should start out slowly with smaller fences and is usually done with fences smaller than the level at which the horse is competing. Particularly in the beginning of a horse's career, he needs to be given the opportunity to become familiar with a lot of different types of fences prior to his first competition; and likewise will need to have done the appropriate amount of schooling before moving up to the next level. It is important that the rider is familiar with the requirements for different levels in order to ask the right questions and develop the correct technique in the horse relevant to each level at which the horse competes.

A lot of the questions such as bounces, doglegs, and fences that require accuracy e.g. corners, and particularly the 'skinny' and accuracy fences, can be practised in an arena. Whilst doing this it is advisable to have wings (rails) on the fences to guide the horse to the fence to begin with so that he learns and understands to go between the flags. The wings should gradually be removed until the horse can jump with confidence a variety of narrow fences and corners.

However, both horse and rider should get used to finding their balance going cross-country where the terrain and the going might vary, where they have to go from a galloping-type fence to a fence that requires more control, and therefore they need to practise the ability to change gear to suit different types of fences. The horse needs to develop the familiarity which would lead to him to be able to jump ditches, water, banks and other natural type fences which he would not be able to see in an arena environment. Horse and rider must learn to judge the correct speed; using a stopwatch is helpful to achieve this.

In order to reach the correct level of fitness for the horse to participate in the cross-country phase he needs to gallop at regular intervals during his training schedule. Again, this should always be done on the best possible surface. Fitness programmes have to be tailored to suit the rider's facilities and type of horse. This work can be done as interval training (see below), in longer, slower sections to build up stamina, or in shorter, faster bursts to build up heart rate and lung capacity i.e. cardiovascular work. Ideally, fast work should be done on a gentle uphill slope as this puts less stress on the horse's limbs. It is worth remembering that during the cross-country competition horses will have to decelerate and accelerate several times during the course in connection with the jumping, and this should be covered during the fitness work where the horse should be asked to change pace at regular intervals.

The warm-up for the cross-country at a competition depends on whether the horse has already done dressage or show jumping during the day, but would usually cover a total period of 30–45 minutes. This would comprise 5–10 minutes walk, 5–10 minutes trot, 2–4 minutes gentle canter with some jumping, a 300–500m sprint plus some fences jumped at near to cross-country speed, 5–15 minutes recovery, including cool down if the weather is hot, and a short trot or canter immediately prior to starting.

Cross-country performed correctly should show horse and rider in harmony, approaching the questions with enthusiasm and flair.

Interval training

This is an alternative to galloping as a means of getting a mature eventer fit. Several short periods of work are alternated with brief recovery periods (the intervals). It is based on methods devised by Jack le Goff (the French trainer who so successfully coached the USA's horse trials teams in the 1970s and 1980s) and adapted from interval-training methods used by athletes.

Principles

- The body will adapt itself to the stress of demands made upon it, as long as it is given time. Therefore repeatedly small but increased demands are made upon it.

- The intervals are timed so that the recovery is not quite achieved before the next period of work.

- The work periods are designed to avoid maximum stress, so that the respiratory, cardiovascular and muscular systems are all gradually developed.

- It is used not more than once every 3 or 4 days as it takes this long for the metabolism to return to normal.

Use

Interval training is only suitable for:

- A mature horse.

- A sound horse.

- A horse who has completed 4 to 8 weeks of basic fittening and conditioning work (i.e. capable of hacking for 1½–2 hours).

6–12 weeks of interval training are needed before a three-day event.

The programme

A programme is devised so that the distance and speeds are gradually increased. A number of competitions can be integrated into the interval-training programme to prepare for a three-day event.

Before cantering, the horse should be warmed-up with 30 minutes of walking and trotting.

After cantering he should be cooled down by gentle work for up to an hour. This is essential to help the vascular system remove waste products accumulated during exercise.

All work must be carried out with the horse going into the bridle and on the aids.

It is essential for the programme to be adjusted to suit the needs of the individual horse. The aspects which can be varied are as follows.

The rest intervals. Range of 1–4 minutes: 4 minutes may be needed for the horse to 'almost' recover at the beginning of training, but only 1 minute if the horse is very fit.

Work periods. These can be varied as follows:

1. Duration: range 3 to 12 minutes, but in total a training session should not be more than 35 minutes.

   NB Excitable horses can be cantered for longer distances more slowly.

2. Number: a maximum of three work periods.

3. Frequency: interval training may be used once to twice a week. With a young horse, once a week might be sufficient, but it is usual to progress to twice a week (every four days).

4. Speeds. These range from trot, through canter to a gallop at about 600m (660yd) per minute. Young horses might begin their interval training with trot periods, but the major part of the work is done at 'half speed' – a canter of approximately 400m (440yd) per minute. As the horse becomes fitter it can be increased to 500m (550yd) per minute and eventually for 800m (½ mile) or 1.6km (1mile) periods at 600m (660yd) per minute

215

NB Horses competing in one- or two-day events before the three-day event need not do faster work until the last two or three weeks. Horses with a history of leg problems should work up hills instead of doing the faster work, and depending on their 'wind' may need one or two pipe-openers, going at close to maximum speed for 500m (550yd) uphill 10 days before the event.

- **Terrain.** If hilly, canter distances can be reduced by up to 25 per cent.

  NB Varied terrain helps to keep the horse fresh.

- **Work on non-cantering days.** If the horse works strongly for 1½ hours on these days, less cantering may be needed. If he does not do much, more may be needed. Work on non-cantering days depends on the particular trainer and is a major cause of differences in cantering programmes.

  NB After a competition a horse will need usually a minimum of 7 days before cantering again.

- **The horse.** The type of horse and how recently he has been fit affects the programme. A small Thoroughbred who has been very fit recently needs less work than a cold-blooded horse who has never been really fit.

Notes on canter work for the event horse

- On approximately the fourth week of basic fittening, start the basic canter work.
- Canter work can be carried out approximately every 4 days; this can be varied slightly to fit in with competitions and other training requirements.
- Prior to any canter work, 20 minutes of continual trot work is needed to warm up the horse; this can include some hill work.
- Some horses benefit from increasing hill work in trot and canter, and decreasing the canter times.
- From the sixth canter workout onwards, it is a good idea to do some work at higher speeds to open up the lungs, for 30–45 seconds during the workout.
- A short trot after the final canter is helpful in letting the horse cool down slowly.

The above are guidelines only.

Evaluating fitness

Heart and respiration rates

- Heart rates can vary, but once a norm has been established a record of the levels and recovery rates of the heart and respiration help in the evaluation of fitness. For an accurate comparison the same amount of exercise and the same intervals after work must be taken. One method is to compare rates every 10 days by cantering up the same hill, stopping, and taking the rates after 1, 5 and 10 minutes. As training progresses, the rates should drop.

- The pulse at rest is normally between 36 and 42 beats per minute and top rate is over 200. For maximum training effect the pulse rate should stay between 100 and 150 while the horse is working.

- Respiration at rest is normally 10 to 16 breaths per minute and it should not go above 100 during work.

- 'False' readings can occur, as an excited horse has a high pulse and a hot horse can respire very quickly. Establish a normal pattern for each individual horse in a given situation.

Feel

It is the experienced eye of the trainer and the feel of the rider which judge the fitness of the horse and his best programme of work. There is no substitute for knowing one's horse, for he is a unique living animal with his own capabilities, limitations and requirements.

Conversion Table

1600m = 1 mile approx.	$1/2$ speed = 400m/min approx.
2400m = $1^1/_2$ miles approx.	$3/_4$ speed = 520m/min approx.
3200m = 2 miles approx.	max speed = 640m/min approx.

The start and finish

The start. This is important, as a quick getaway can save valuable seconds. Practise walking into a start box or similar area.

Keeping quite calm, walk in a small circle until the starter begins the countdown at 5 seconds. Walk into the box and face away from the exit. Quietly turn round so that the horse is ready and does not get upset. The rider should not fight the exuberant horse. He will settle far more quickly if the rider sits quite still and keeps a firm contact on the reins.

The finish. After passing the finish keep hold of the horse's head and bring him gradually to a walk. Flopping in on a loose rein at speed is foolish, as tired horses easily break down if they stumble.

Safety equipment

Safety when jumping cross-country cannot be stressed too strongly. For the horse, overreach boots, brushing boots, surcingle and a breast plate are strongly advised. Studs should be used behind, and in front if the going is slippery. For the rider, a crash hat and body protector are compulsory in eventing and cross-country competitions.

Summary

The need for patience and thoughtful training cannot be over-stressed: they are essential in the education of a young horse. If time is spent in the beginning gradually increasing the ability and confidence of the horse, the outcome should be rewarded by many happy hours riding across country in what is a thrilling and most exciting aspect of equestrian sport.

Index